BE NEAR ME, LORD JESUS

DEVOTIONS FOR THE ADVENT AND CHRISTMAS SEASONS

Richard E. Lauersdorf

Northwestern Publishing House
Milwaukee, Wisconsin

Second printing, 2006

Library of Congress Control Number: 2002108323
Northwestern Publishing House
1250 N. 113th St., Milwaukee, WI 53226-3284
© 2002 by Northwestern Publishing House
Published 2002
Printed in the United States of America
ISBN 978-0-8100-1489-3

To Charlene–
my partner in kneeling
at Jesus' manger bed

TABLE OF CONTENTS

Waiting and Watching

Author's Preface vii

December 1 . . . . . Locked Out No Longer 1

December 2 . . . . . The Right Kind of Seed 5

December 3 . . . . . A Knot-Free Branch 9

December 4 . . . . . Don't Miss the Baby 12

December 5 . . . . . Why Bethlehem? 16

December 6 . . . . . Still Waiting? 20

December 7 . . . . . Getting or Giving? 24

December 8 . . . . . Isn't That a Wonderful Baby? 28

December 9 . . . . . Who's Coming to Our House? . . . 32

December 10 . . . . Advice for Advent 36

December 11 . . . . We're Listening, John 40

December 12 . . . . A Family Christmas 44

Unwrapping and Wondering

December 13 . . . That's Our Song 48

December 14 . . . What Are We Getting from
Christmas? 52

December 15 . . . Building Up Faith's Muscles 56

December 16 . . . Front Row Seats 60

December 17 . . . Love's Pure Light 64

December 18 . . . Can You See the Light? 68

December 19 . . . Get a Life! 72

December 20 . . . A Piece of That Peace 76

December 21 . . . A Word We Can See 80

December 22 . . . I Hope So? or I Know So! 84

December 23 . . . Have Yourself a Merry
                   Big Christmas 87

Worshiping and Witnessing

December 24 . . . It's Time to Think about Names . . . 91

December 25 . . . Our Best Christmas Gift. 95

December 26 . . . Christmas Still Today 99

December 27 . . . Don't Switch Off Jesus!. 103

December 28 . . . An Endless Christmas 106

December 29 . . . We Got the Gift;
                  He Gets the Praise 110

December 30 . . . Connecting the Everlasting 114

December 31 . . . Nothing's Changed 118

January 1 . . . . . . An Old Name for a New Year. 121

January 2 . . . . . . Mary's Scrapbook 125

January 3 . . . . . . Holding or Held? 129

January 4 . . . . . . Worshiper and Witness 133

January 5 . . . . . . We Want to Be in That Number . . . 137

January 6 . . . . . . A Word from the Wise 141

AUTHOR'S PREFACE

Some things stick in our minds! Like the stanza from "Away in a Manger" many of us learned as children, teach to our children, and sing with our grandchildren.

Be near me, Lord Jesus; I ask you to stay
Close by me forever and love me, I pray.
Bless all the dear children in your tender care,
And take us to heaven to live with you there.
(*Christian Worship* [CW] 68:3)

Simple words. But they summarize well the deep meaning of Advent and Christmas. God himself drew *near us* to bridge the impossible gap between sinful human beings and himself. On Christmas Day he sent his Son into the manger. And so began his journey to the cross. Day after day God's Spirit enters our hearts to make them manger beds for the Christ Child. On the Last Day, God's Son will come again to take us to heaven to live with him there. Only God can show such great love and do such great things.

During the Advent and Christmas seasons, God's children of all ages take time to marvel at his love and to renew their prayer, "Be near me, Lord Jesus." May God use this little book of devotions to aid them.

Richard E. Lauersdorf

After he drove the man out, he placed on the east side of the Garden of Eden cherubim and a flaming sword flashing back and forth to guard the way to the tree of life. (Genesis 3:24)

LOCKED OUT NO LONGER

Ever been locked out? After a hurried trip to the grocery store, my wife and I drove into our garage only to discover that neither of us had a house key. I had to preach that Saturday evening. The service was set to begin in an hour, and my robe and my sermon were still in the house. Do you know how hard a basement window is to break when you're actually trying to? And how difficult it is to squeeze through such a narrow opening? What a feeling!

Adam and Eve were locked out—locked out of the Garden of Eden. And they had no one to blame but themselves. For no good reason, they doubted God's word, disobeyed his command, and ditched him for his archenemy, the prince of hell. With their sin they slammed shut the door of a wondrous, heavenlike existence with their

Maker. Who could have blamed God if he had turned his back on them and in righteous anger declared, "If that's the way you want it, so be it"? Or who could have shouted "Unfair!" if, with fiery wrath, he had reached down to make a smoking spot of carbon out of them, right there in the garden.

There was no basement window for Adam and Eve to crawl through. Ahead of them lay only a locked-out existence—filled with fearful hiding from a righteous God, fixing the blame on each other, facing "ashes to ashes" on earth and a fiery end in a forever hell. Locked out—they knew the feeling!

Our first parents didn't want to leave their nice home; God had to drive them out. He even put a guard with a flashing, flaming sword in front of the door. He did this in his love—though Adam and Eve perhaps didn't recognize it as such—for he didn't want them to eat of the tree of life and live on forever in their sin-stained condition. In a love that only God could display, he had other plans for them. And he announced those plans in the first promise of the Savior—the seed of the woman, who would crush Satan's head. Through that Savior, Adam and Eve would once again enjoy perfect fellowship with him in heaven. There they would "eat from the tree of life, which is in the paradise of God" (Revelation 2:7).

How eagerly Adam and Eve must have waited and watched for the Savior to come! Some have even translated Eve's words at the birth of their first child as "I have gotten a man, the Lord" (Genesis 4:1)—though that son turned out to be the first murderer instead of the promised Savior.

One wonders: Did they ever pass near the Garden of Eden again without sadly remembering how their sin had slammed the door on so much more than their earthly home? Or as each day passed, did they raise expectant eyes to heaven, looking for the One who would open the door back to their Father—both here on earth and in heaven? For them life must have been one continuous advent of waiting and watching for the promised Savior's coming.

What about us? Are we too watching and waiting for his coming. Or has Advent lost its "punch" for us? Do we approach it with a sort of "ho-hum, we've been here before" feeling? Is all the watching and waiting of Advent anticlimactic because we've had Jesus as the key to heaven's door for as long as we can remember? Then perhaps we ought to stand outside of our locked house door some midnight and pound and pound with no way to get in.

Even better, each day of the Advent season, let's reconsider the bitter legacy our first parents left us—and which we've earned for ourselves. Sin has more than double locked and dead bolted heaven's door. It's made it impossible for us to break our way in, or even want to. Only God's Son is the way. Only the promised and then sent

3

Savior can say, "I am the gate; whoever enters through me will be saved" (John 10:9).

For his coming Adam and Eve waited and watched. Because of his coming, we rejoice and celebrate.

For us he opens wide the door of
paradise today. The angel guards the gate
no more; to God our thanks we pay. Amen.
(CW 41:6)

2
DEC

And I will put enmity between you and the woman, and between your offspring [NIV footnote: seed] and hers; he will crush your head, and you will strike his heel. (Genesis 3:15)

THE RIGHT KIND OF SEED

It was the first time I had helped my father plant the garden. My job was to hand him the seed packets from the wooden box in which he had stored them. The packets were all the same color and had no illustrations on them. "Hand me the carrot seed," he said, straightening up from the row he had opened. And I gave him the first packet my little fingers found. "No," he said, looking at the packet, "dill seed won't do. You need the right kind of seed."

What a day that must have been for our first parents in the Garden of Eden. The odor of disobedience, despair, and death hung heavy in the air. No longer could they walk with God. Now they scurried away in fright and hid from him. No longer were they friends of God. Now they were his enemies. No longer would they live forever

5

with him. Now they would spend eternity with the devil, who had deceived them. What were they to do? Where could they turn?

That's when the Lord in his love and grace came to them. First, he confronted Adam and Eve with their sin. Then he comforted them with the first promise of the Savior. In that promise he spoke of seed—not just any kind of seed but the seed of the woman. Through Eve, Satan had brought sin and death into the world. Through her offspring, God would conquer sin, death, and Satan.

Note the completeness already in this first gospel promise. The conqueror would come from the woman; nothing is said about the man. The Savior would be virgin born, and he would win the victory. The battle would be fierce. The cross would be splintery against his skin. The fires of hell would sear his soul. But in the end, this heavenly seed of the woman would grind Satan's head into the dust of defeat. With this loving promise, God whisked away the pall of despair and death that hung over the garden that day. Because of this loving promise, Adam and Eve could look forward to the eternal day.

Want Advent to be meaningful? Want it to be filled with awe and wonder? Then think about seed again—not just any kind of seed but the right kind. Where would we be without that seed of the woman? Right back where Adam and Eve were before a loving Lord came looking for them in the garden. Like them, we'd be trying to ignore him—

at least as far as our consciences would allow us to. Or perhaps we'd sit there shivering at the thought of God's judgment. Or perhaps we'd be pointing our fingers at someone or something else—trying to shift the blame for our sins. But such stratagems only work so long. Sooner or later the truth catches up with us—if not here on earth, then in eternity, in the final judgment, which will be conducted by a just and holy God.

"Hand me the right kind of seed," is our Advent prayer. Let me see, up close and clearly, the Savior, *my* Savior, born of Eve's descendant. Let me marvel again at the love that bared him to the schemes of Satan, burdened him with my sins, bruised his heel on the shameful cross. Above all, let me marvel at the victory he has brought me. No longer is Satan my erstwhile friend, as he was for that brief moment with Eve in the garden. Though he may still sidle up to me and purr like some kitten, he always ends up trying to use his claws on my soul. But now I know him as my enemy.

And now I know how to defeat him—by standing close to Jesus, the seed of the woman. And since I'm one of Eve's offspring, there will always be an ongoing conflict between me and Satan's followers. But now the world doesn't have to win. I can—again by standing close to Jesus, the seed of the woman. And when the eternal advent comes, what victory will be mine as I enter into perfect oneness with God in heaven. Yes, it will be *my* victory—but only because Jesus, the seed of the woman, will be standing next to me.

For the coming of that precious seed, Adam and Eve waited and watched. Because of his coming, we rejoice and celebrate.

Crush for me the serpent's head that, set free from doubt and dread, I may cling to you in faith, safely kept through life and death. Amen. (CW 28:5)

"The days are coming," declares the Lord, *"when I will raise up to David a righteous Branch."* *(Jeremiah 23:5)*

A KNOT-FREE BRANCH

Ever try to find a piece of lumber without any knots or defects? I went through piece after piece of 1" x 4" pine at the lumberyard and didn't find a single one that was perfect. Neither was my workmanship perfect—I have to admit—as I fashioned those boards into a Lenten-Easter cross we could light up on our front porch.

Some six hundred years before Bethlehem became the cradle of Christ, Jeremiah spoke about knot-free lumber and perfect workmanship. What the Lord said through his prophet about this "righteous Branch" helps prepare our hearts for Christ's coming this Advent season.

And what a mouthful God gave Jeremiah. The Lord had told Israel repeatedly that the promised Savior would be great David's greater Son. But years had gone by, and David's line, by Jeremiah's time, seemed like some decaying tree snapped off just above the ground. To the outward eye, only a rotting stump remained—a stump from which only mushrooms and weeds could come. "Not so," said the Lord, "watch that stump, for from it will come the Branch I have promised—my Son sent into human flesh to save my people from their sins."

Anything noteworthy for us in this truth for this Advent season? Many of us, with our eyes closed, can recite that Mary was of "the house and line of David," as was her husband Joseph (Luke 2:4). We've been reminded again and again how God flexed his omniscience and omnipotence to turn history's wheels, so that Rome decreed a census and Mary and Joseph journeyed to David's ancestral city. A Branch raised up to David—yes, we know all about that.

And yet because of the comforting truth behind it all, we need to hear it again. Our Lord is a perfect workman. Everything he says, he does. When he promises a Branch from David's line, he means it. When he threatens to plunge the unbeliever into an unending hell, he means it. When he offers eternal life to all who believe in his Son, he means it. When, through that Savior, he holds out comfort for those who mourn, help for those who struggle, friendship for the lonely, understanding for the perplexed, he means it. "Look again at that Branch of David in the Bethlehem manger," Jeremiah's prophecy reminds us, "and be assured that the Lord always works out his promises."

Jeremiah's prophecy tells us something else, something so miraculous we can hardly believe it. This Branch from David would be "righteous"—perfectly holy, without any sin of any kind. Every other descendant of David had to join his ancestral father in confessing, "Surely I have been a sinner from birth, sinful from the time my mother conceived me" (Psalm 51:5). But this special Branch would be "holy, blameless, pure, set apart from sinners" (Hebrews 7:26). Yes, he would be in a class all by himself, with no knots or defects in him.

Anything noteworthy for us in this truth for this Advent season? Not if we haven't looked at ourselves lately to see how soiled and spotted by sin we are. Not if we haven't looked closely at that righteous Branch from David's line and seen why he came. Not if we fail to remember that not his sin but ours put him on the accursed tree. Not his guilt but ours plunged him into hell's torments. Not his salvation but ours he came to prepare. This Advent season, may the Lord help us marvel anew at the amazing love behind the righteous Branch he raised up to David.

For the coming of this righteous Branch, Jeremiah waited and watched. Because of his coming, we rejoice and celebrate.

Hail, hosanna, David's Son! Help, Lord; hear our supplication! Let your kingdom, scepter, crown bring us blessing and salvation that forever we may sing Hail, hosanna! to our King. Amen. (CW 8:4)

11

"The days are coming," declares the L*ORD,* *"when I will raise up to David a righteous Branch, a King who will reign wisely and do what is just and right in the land. In his days Judah will be saved and Israel will live in safety. This is the name by which he will be called: The* L*ORD* *Our Righteousness."* (*Jeremiah 23:5,6*)

DON'T MISS THE BABY

"Where's the baby?" asked little Amie. On the way into church for the Christmas Eve service, the family had stopped before the manger scene set up on the lawn. Everything was in place. The church custodian had anchored the manger, covered the ground with straw, positioned Mary and Joseph around the small wooden crib, and placed the shepherds in just the right spot. But something was missing. And all week long the people had gone by that manger scene and never noticed. The Christ Child wasn't there. They had missed the most important part.

This holiday season many will miss the Christ Child as they chase after and get caught up in what the world calls Christmas. The danger is always there that we might join them. That's why we need the Lord's words through Jeremiah—so that we don't miss the most important part of Christmas.

Miss the Christ Child? How can we when we stop to consider what he brings us? Some six centuries before the miracle of Bethlehem, God told his people, Judah, what the marvelous Branch from David's stem would bring. He even piled up the words so that there could be no misunderstanding. "A King who will reign wisely," he said. The King from David's royal line would know God's saving will perfectly, agree with it fully, and carry it out completely.

This heavenly King would "do"—that is, "establish"—what is just and right in the land. Not only would he be righteous and holy in his own person, but he would also prepare perfect righteousness and holiness for others. That's why he was called "The LORD Our Righteousness." In making full payment for our sins, great David's greater Son would wash us clean and make us whiter than snow in the eyes of a holy God. By keeping all the commandments perfectly, he would weave a robe of righteousness for us to wear before our holy judge in heaven. The Lord Our Righteousness— what a name for this child!

With the words "In his days Judah will be saved and Israel will live in safety," the Lord repeats the thought. This was not a promise that the children of Judah in Christ's day would once again have their political independence and dwell safely in an *earthly* land called Palestine. Quite the contrary—the last three centuries before Bethlehem's manger would turn out to be ones of constant warfare and cruel oppression. Rather, the Lord here was speaking of his true Judah, his *spiritual* Israel—all those true believers in Jesus Christ—and the spiritual blessings that would be theirs in the Christ Child. Righteousness and salvation, peace and safety for the soul—these are the blessings Christ brings.

Anything new here for us? Ask what Jesus has brought and what Jesus should mean, and many of us would answer: "He brings salvation. He is the Savior." But those tremendous words can become so commonplace, so taken for granted—like the air we breathe and the heart beating inside our chest—that the Christ Child barely makes it into our Christmas scenes.

Some avid walkers carry a device that counts the feet and miles they cover. Too bad we don't have a device that would count the missteps we sinners take each day—whether in thought, word, or deed. Advent, then, is the time to try to tally up our sinfulness. For only when we do so will our souls cry out in their abject need for the Lord Our Righteousness.

And what about the peace he brings? "Come on," the Lord tells us through Jeremiah. "You who are lonely or lost, you who are sorrowing or suffering, don't just sit there in your gloom. Turn to the

Christ Child, kneel before his crib and cross. There's peace and safety to be found in him."

Miss the baby? For his coming, true Israel of Jeremiah's day waited and watched. Because of his coming, we rejoice and celebrate.

Come, O long-expected Jesus, born to set your people free; from our sins and fears release us by your death on Calvary. Israel's Strength and Consolation, hope to all the earth impart, dear Desire of ev'ry nation, joy of ev'ry longing heart. Amen. (CW 6:1)

5 DEC

But you, Bethlehem Ephrathah, though you are small among the clans of Judah, out of you will come for me one who will be ruler over Israel. (Micah 5:2)

WHY BETHLEHEM?

Magazines periodically publish lists of the best and worst cities in which to live. Some years ago *Money* magazine surveyed three hundred cities and ranked Bethlehem, Pennsylvania, dead last. Makes one wonder where the survey would have placed Bethlehem, Judea. If the people had been given the choice of where the King of kings would be born, would Bethlehem in Judea have even made the list? Yet that's where the miracle of the ages occurred, just as the prophet Micah had foretold seven hundred years earlier. Why Bethlehem?

If Jerusalem had been the choice, we could understand. It was the nation's capital, its largest city, the center of commerce and political power, the site of God's temple—it certainly stood out among all the cities of Palestine. But Bethlehem—that little farming and sheep-raising village five miles down the road from mighty Jerusalem—why that little burg? Bethlehem was such a small town that it didn't even rank with the clans of Judah. Judah—as all the other tribes of Israel—was divided into sections with one thousand families each. This made for easy and effective governing. Each section then had its ranking official. But Bethlehem was the least among these clan cities; its headman was not even numbered among the rulers of Judah.

If there were historical markers in those days, several would have dotted Bethlehem's landscape. Near the village itself, Jacob's wife Rachel had died giving birth to their second son—whom she had fittingly named Benjamin, that is, "son of my sorrow." There Jacob had buried Rachel, the woman he had loved so dearly that he spent 14 years at hard labor in order that he might have her as his wife. In Bethlehem's fields Ruth, one of the Savior's ancestors, had gleaned the grain left behind by the harvesters. And most important of all, David, Israel's illustrious king, had been born in this little town. Such events gave little Bethlehem at least a bit of recognition.

Yet Micah predicted a far more important event for the little town of Bethlehem—one that history would mark forever. "Out of you will come for me," Micah quotes the Lord as saying, "one who will be ruler over Israel." From this little town would come one far greater than the person regarded as its most illustrious citizen—King

David. He who ruled over an earthly Israel would be a midget compared to this King who was coming. This King would rule over true Israel—that kingdom of all true believers who from all times and places and languages and colors would belong to God and stand with him in all eternity. That's who was coming from Bethlehem!

But why Bethlehem? Why this insignificant town for such a significant birth? Could it be that God chose Bethlehem because he was thinking of us, of you and me? For how significant are we? Who of us—in spite of what we may dream of at times—is going to have his or her name written in the history books? Even some of our country's presidents might not be remembered if teachers hadn't made sure to drill their names into our heads in history classes. Is there a lesson for insignificant entities like you and me in God's choice of Bethlehem for the Savior's birth?

Yes! This Christmas season let each of us—as we hear and sing about the little town of Bethlehem once again—understand that not a single one of us is insignificant in God's eyes. He wants each one of us. His heart beats in love for each of us. He sent his Son into that crib and onto that cross to save each of us, to save you and me. Others may belittle and poke fun at us, but not our God. He reaches down to us. Others may stand taller in the world's opinion than we do. But our God, through his Son, elevates each of us to the rank of sons and daughters in his eternal family and grants us visas into his kingdom. The devil may try to use our consciences to discredit us and hold our sins against us, but Bethlehem tells us again and again that peace with God is still there for us. Just as he did with insignificant Bethlehem, so our loving God has done something wondrously significant for the insignificant, for you and for me.

For the coming of this King of kings to the little town of Bethlehem, Micah waited and watched. Because of his coming, each one of us can rejoice and celebrate.

Since all he comes to ransom, by all be he adored, the infant born in Bethl'em, the Savior and the Lord. Repeat the hymn again: "To God on high be glory and peace on earth to men." Amen. (CW 36:4)

6 DEC

He will stand and shepherd his flock in the strength of the LORD, in the majesty of the name of the LORD his God. And they will live securely, for then his greatness will reach to the ends of the earth. And he will be their peace. (Micah 5:4,5)

STILL WAITING?

Close your eyes for a moment. Try to imagine what Bethlehem was like at the time of Christ's birth. Widen your scope to include the world around that little town. Think they were much different from our towns and our world? Were their homes teeming with joy or rife with bitterness? Were their streets clean and safe or dirty and dangerous? Were the nations of that era set on global cooperation, or were they unwilling to talk or work together? You see, the centuries and the circumstances may have changed, but the need for the Savior's coming has not changed. There's a world out there still waiting for what the babe of Bethlehem brings. So are we.

So what will the babe of Bethlehem bring us this Christmas? Familiarity can dim our appreciation for the gifts Jesus brings. It can even dull our expectation for Jesus himself. Without even realizing it, we may treat him much like pizza in our freezer—no longer special but something always there and, as a result, less valued. "Wake up," Micah would tell us. "The babe of Bethlehem, your Shepherd, is coming. He will care for you as a member of his flock with the strength of the Lord."

Now, a shepherd doesn't *rule* his flock by force, by whipping his flock into submission. Instead, he *rules with a loving concern*—a concern that the sheep soon recognize has their well-being at heart.

Now look at the babe of Bethlehem. How strong is his love and concern for us. His love brought him into the manger at Bethlehem to do for us what we couldn't do for ourselves. As our Good Shepherd, he came to lay down his life for us, to pay for our sins with his life's blood. Those little hands stirring around in Bethlehem's manger were later stretched out on Calvary's cross for you and for me. Through his gospel they still reach down to us each new day with this invitation: Give me your sins. That's what I came for. "Give me those daily sins. Give me those almost forgotten ones and those always remembered ones. Give them to me because I have the strength—the strength of the Lord—to take care of them. Indeed, on Calvary's cross I already have." Are we waiting for the Lord Jesus, our strong Shepherd, anxiously and joyously this Advent season? I hope so. We need him so much.

What else does the marvelous babe of Bethlehem bring us? "Majesty," Micah answered. *Majesty* stands for his greatness, his glory, his beauty. What a strange way Jesus had of showing that majesty. It led him from a throne of splendor into the poorest crib imaginable, a manger full of straw. It surrounded him with our skin and saddled him with our sins. It brought him right into the midst of people who needed his mercy and help. And he didn't disappoint them.

Nor will he disappoint us! If we look only at our troubles this Advent season, there will be little joy. "Raise those eyes," Micah would tell us. "Raise them to the One who brings you triumph over trouble. Wait for him—you who are sorely tried and troubled by your own or a loved one's illness. Wait for him—you who have families where parents can't get along and children don't obey. Wait for him— you whose loved ones are gone and only memories remain. Wait for him—you who feel lonely and unloved. Wait for him—you who don't know where to turn or whom to trust. Wait for him—you who think you have more troubles than there are solutions. The babe of Bethlehem will shepherd you in the majesty of the name of the Lord his God. He will lead you and feed you, and you can dwell securely. He will be your peace—the peace that truly transcends all understanding and that no circumstance or trouble can ever take from you."

Close your eyes again. Picture your neighborhood, your town, your country, your world. So many are still waiting for God's great good news, still waiting for someone to tell them what the babe of Bethlehem brings. So many, in short, are still waiting *for us!*

Micah, as he waited and watched for the Savior's coming, told us about the babe of Bethlehem, of him who would come to "stand and shepherd his flock in the strength of the LORD." Now may God, as we rejoice and celebrate, use us to tell others of the One who has come.

O holy Child of Bethlehem, descend to us, we pray; cast out our sin and enter in; be born in us today. We hear the Christmas angels the great glad tidings tell; oh, come to us, abide with us, our Lord Immanuel! Amen. (CW 65:4)

*In that day you will say: "I will praise you,
O Lord. Although you were angry with me, your
anger has turned away and you have comforted me.
Surely God is my salvation; I will trust and not be
afraid. The Lord, the Lord, is my strength and my
song; he has become my salvation." In that day
you will say: "Give thanks to the Lord, call on his
name; make known among the nations what he has
done, and proclaim that his name is exalted."
(Isaiah 12:1,2,4)*

GETTING OR GIVING?

One minute my four-year-old son, eyes wide in
anticipation, was tearing the wrapping paper off
the Christmas present I had just handed to him.
The next minute he was hurrying toward my chair,
watching for my reaction to the present he had for
me. What's Christmas for—getting or giving?
"Both," Isaiah reminded Judah—and also us.

Seven centuries before Christ's birth in Bethlehem, God had sent Isaiah to warn his wayward
children that if they continued in their heedless
forsaking of him, punishment would come. And

24

it did, a century later. The armies of Babylon marched into Judah and carted the people off into captivity.

But those words of doom were only half of Isaiah's message. The other half were words of comfort—a promise that God's anger would be turned aside and that he, as their Savior, would deliver them. The faithful in Judah understood that this deliverance included not only deliverance from Babylon but deliverance from sin, death, and the devil. That's why Isaiah sang, "The LORD, the LORD, is my strength and my song; he has become my salvation."

Do you feel Isaiah's joy as he anticipated "getting" from Christmas? It's almost as if he were there seven hundred years later when Mary, pregnant with the Christ Child, told Elizabeth, "My soul glorifies the Lord and my spirit rejoices in God my Savior" (Luke 1:46,47). Or when Zechariah, holding his eight-day-old son, John, exclaimed, "Praise be to the Lord . . . because he has come and has redeemed his people" (Luke 1:68). Or when Simeon, feeling the heartbeat of the seven-week-old Savior, sang, "Sovereign Lord, as you have promised, you now dismiss your servant in peace, for my eyes have seen your salvation" (Luke 2:29,30).

Dr. Gordon Alles helped develop insulin as a treatment for diabetes—only to die later of the disease because he didn't even know he had it. The more we recognize sin's disease, the more we'll rejoice in the cure God has prepared for us. Advent is a time to look more deeply and to see more clearly how our thoughts, words, and deeds show up on God's X-ray screen. Christmas is for *getting*, Isaiah reminds us: getting the one and only cure for our sins, getting the best God has to give—our salvation.

Christmas is also for *giving*. "Give thanks to the LORD," Isaiah urged Judah, "make known among the nations what he has done." Do you feel his joy as he connected giving with Christmas? It's almost as if he were there that night, walking behind those shepherds as they, with unbridled joy, "spread the word concerning what had been told them about this child" (Luke 2:17). It's almost as if he were there that day in the temple, watching as the aged widow Anna "spoke about the child to all who were looking forward to the redemption of Jerusalem" (Luke 2:38). And it's almost as if he were there along the banks of the Jordan River that morning, as joyous Andrew rushed to tell his brother Simon, "We have found the Messiah" (John 1:41).

What would Isaiah notice if he were to step among us today? Would it be the same reaction, the same joyous desire to give to others what has been given to us? Is there some wayward family member, some unchurched neighbor, some unknown person on the other side of the world, waiting for a Christmas present from us? There's joy to be found in giving Christ for Christmas.

Those who make known among the nations what the Lord has done will find their own joy increased.

Watch your children or grandchildren this Christmas. Christmas is for *getting* and for *giving* the greatest present of all time. For his coming, Isaiah waited and watched. Because of his coming, we rejoice and celebrate.

We are rich, for he was poor; is not this a wonder? Therefore praise God evermore here on earth and yonder. Amen. (CW 64:3)

8 DEC

Therefore the Lord himself will give you a sign: The virgin will be with child and will give birth to a son, and will call him Immanuel. (Isaiah 7:14)

ISN'T THAT A WONDERFUL BABY?

Standing with his buddies before the hospital's nursery window, the new father pointed to his firstborn son and said, "Isn't that a wonderful baby?" Every baby is—regardless of how mottled or clear its skin is, regardless of how much hair it has or doesn't have. How wise God's love is to bring human beings into the world the way that he does. How rich the miracle he packs into each one of those babies.

Seven hundred years before it actually happened, God's prophet Isaiah takes us not to a nursery window but to a manger in Bethlehem. The newborn baby, asleep there on the hay, is truly wonderful.

Why is he such a wonderful baby? Because he would be born of a virgin. We don't need to dig into a lot of Hebrew dictionaries to show that the word Isaiah used actually meant "virgin." All we have to do is read on and let Scripture explain itself. Remember Mary's question when the angel told her that she would be the Christ Child's mother: "How will this be . . . since I am a virgin?" (Luke 1:34). Better still, remember the angel's answer: "The Holy Spirit will come upon you, and the power of the Most High will overshadow you. So the holy one to be born will be called the Son of God" (Luke 1:35). Joseph, troubled by the news of his fiancée's pregnancy, received the same answer. In fact, the angel even quoted Isaiah's words to him: "The virgin will be with child and will give birth to a son, and they will call him Immanuel" (Matthew 1:23).

There's no other baby like him! Every other child is flesh born of flesh, with a sinful heart inherited from a sinful father and mother. Mary's son, conceived in her by the Holy Spirit, would be the Holy One. Every other child faces death as the wage of his or her sin. Mary's sinless child would die not to pay for his own sin but for the world's sin. Let the "show me," rational world in which we have to live disdain that which logic cannot touch and trace. For us, reason gives way to revelation and logic gives way to faith. The *how* of his virgin birth is far beyond us, but we believe it because Scripture says it. Far more important for us is to understand the *why*. Only the sinless Son of God could have blood precious enough to cover all our sins.

Why is he such a wonderful baby? Because his name would fit him. He is Immanuel, which means "God with us." He who promised "I will be their God" (Jeremiah 31:33) now comes not in power or might but in the birth of a little baby. There in the manger, we see eternity squeezed into time, the infinite packaged into history. That little one, scarcely able to hold up his head, is the almighty God who holds the world together. That little one, rocked in his mother's arms, is the Lord, who rules heaven and earth. That little one, nursing at his mother's breast, is the one who gives every living creature what it needs. "How?" we ask. "How can this be, God in human flesh?" The *how* is far beyond us, but we believe it because Scripture says so. Far more important, once again, is to understand the *why.*

A wonderful baby indeed. So wonderful we will want to take the time this Advent season to join Isaiah on our knees before the manger bed of our Immanuel. Me—a sinner who didn't desire him, who didn't deserve him, whose only thought was to disdain him—he, my God, came down to earth into human form to save. Me—a sinner he loved so much and with such a desire to save that he tasted hunger and thirst, loneliness and grief. For me he was falsely accused by the enemy and denied and betrayed by his friends. For me he was forsaken by his Father. For me he felt the divine wrath I deserved for my sin. For me he experienced pain and suffering and agony. For me he wore a crown of thorns and bore a cross of shame. For me and my sins he gave up his own life as a ransom. For me he filled the grave. And from that grave, he arose to declare that I have been redeemed fully and forever. How can we say Immanuel without marveling at the awesome love behind that miracle?

Whisper that wonderful name. Shout it! He is near. He is real. He is yours. He is mine. He is "God with us."

For the coming of that wonderful baby, Isaiah waited and watched. Because Immanuel has come, we rejoice and celebrate.

Enter now my waiting heart, glorious King and Lord most holy. Dwell in me and ne'er depart, though I am but poor and lowly. Ah, what riches will be mine when you are my guest divine. Amen. (CW 8:2)

"See, I will send my messenger, who will prepare the way before me. Then suddenly the Lord you are seeking will come to his temple; the messenger of the covenant, whom you desire, will come," says the LORD *Almighty. (Malachi 3:1)*

WHO'S COMING TO OUR HOUSE?

Will they all make it this Christmas season? Will our grown children, scattered across the states or throughout the world, come home for Christmas? What a joyous time that will be! Grandchildren wonder too. Will Grandpa and Grandma make it to their Christmas Eve service? What presents will they be bringing? Happy hearts can hardly wait for loved ones to come.

Malachi was waiting for the first Christmas to come. Though he didn't live to see the Christ Child in the manger of Bethlehem, he did write about the joy the Savior would bring.

"He's coming," Malachi told the people of his day. Many of them had forgotten the promise of the Savior's coming or figured it was of little importance. But the prophet, guided by the Holy

Spirit, saw it coming. It would still be four hundred years before John the Baptist would stand on the banks of the Jordan with his message of repentance and baptism of forgiveness to prepare the people. But it would happen. And suddenly the Savior would stand there in the midst of the temple, his people. What a message Malachi had for them—a message of joy because of who was coming to their hearts and homes for Christmas.

Notice who the prophet said was coming. "The Lord," he wrote. The one who came to Bethlehem in Judah and who wants to come to our hearts and homes is the Lord himself. That baby is the faithful God who makes and keeps all his promises. Above all, he is the loving God who makes and keeps his promise of salvation. Our Christmas joy comes not from looking at a sweet little baby asleep on the hay but from looking at a faithful God, who always does what he says he will. As we kneel at that manger, we look at the miracle of the ages—the Lord come into our flesh—and we just have to sing, "Joy to the world, the Lord is come."

Notice what else the prophet called the coming One: "The messenger of the covenant." To what covenant was Malachi referring? Surely not the law, of which God had stated, "This do and you will live." Sinners feel no desire for and find little delight in the commands of God that only condemn them and consign them to an eternity in hell. For a messenger of such a covenant, Judah would hardly throw open its doors in delight. Nor would we.

The covenant of which the prophet spoke was the wonderful one-sided agreement our gracious God made with our first parents in the Garden of Eden. To sin-ruined Adam and Eve, he spoke of the "seed of the woman" coming to crush Satan's head. Again and again over the centuries, God repeated his promise of the Savior, calling him "the Star over Israel," "the Branch out of Jesse," "the Rest Bringer," "the Virgin's Son," "the Prince of Peace." Now it was Malachi's turn. "You know who's coming," Malachi told his people, "the Messenger of the covenant, the Savior who will fulfill God's covenant by paying for all your sins."

If that news doesn't make us sing this Christmas, we might as well turn off the lights on the tree and cancel the family gatherings. Why go through all the bother? But if we know that Christmas is about our Savior's coming, then all the rest of the celebrating has extra meaning. Then our family coming together means sharing true joy as fellow members of God's family through our brother and Savior Jesus Christ. Then the gifts we bring are seasoned with the joy that comes from the greatest gift of all—God's Son—who came to be our Redeemer, our joy, and our delight. Then the special worship services we attend are viewed as extra opportunities in which to adore him who is Christ the Lord.

Who's coming to our house this Christmas? For the coming of his Lord and Savior, Malachi waited and watched. Because of his coming, we rejoice and celebrate.

Now sing we, now rejoice, now raise to heav'n our voice; he from whom joy streameth poor in a manger lies; not so brightly beameth the sun in yonder skies. Thou my Savior art! Thou my Savior art! Amen. (CW 34:1)

10 DEC

"Surely the day is coming; it will burn like a furnace. All the arrogant and every evildoer will be stubble, and that day that is coming will set them on fire," says the LORD Almighty. "Not a root or a branch will be left to them. But for you who revere my name, the sun of righteousness will rise with healing in its wings." (Malachi 4:1,2)

ADVICE FOR ADVENT

Advice is easier to give than to take. Wise parents know this and learn how to counsel their growing children who are about to embark down that road called "the future." Maturing children also grow wise and learn how to listen to parents who have traveled life's road before them. And when the heavenly Father gives advice to his children about heaven's road, the wise ones listen and follow. In the last chapter of the last Old Testament book, the Lord used his prophet Malachi to offer some wholesome Advent advice.

For almost a week the fire blazed along the freeway. When it was burned out, there was practically nothing left. The grass, which the highway department used to cut, was powdery black ash. The pine trees were gone—some of them totally, and others were charred wrecks, never to grow again.

That's what Malachi said would happen to arrogant evildoers. Those who haughtily flip aside God's Word, who feel no need for God's promised Savior, who spend their days in total disregard for God's commands, will face a rude awakening. There's a day coming, filled with judgment more full and final than any consuming brush fire. That day, like some traveler, is already underway and will arrive at the Lord's appointed time. And when it comes—the last day of the world or a person's last day in the world—those who fail to listen to the Lord will find out that he always means what he says. "Surely the day is coming" is no idle threat!

Does it seem odd that Malachi, in the last chapter of the last book written before Christ's coming to the manger, should speak about Christ's coming on the Last Day? Not really. Malachi, as well as the other prophets, saw all of God's acts as one grand event. It's something like looking at the mountains from a distance. Peak after peak stand side by side, touching each other. It's only when you drive closer that you realize how much distance exists between those peaks. Malachi, from his distant point of view, saw Christ's advent in the manger and his advent on the Last Day side by side. We today see some of the miles between those two great events.

But we dare not separate the two advents. If we do, the Christ in the manger will be little more to us than a sweet little baby asleep on the hay. We'll never truly know him unless we link his manger bed with his cross of pain, his emptied tomb, his mount of ascension, and his return in glory. Only then will we be ready for that day that is truly coming.

How long a troubled night can seem. The mind broods over major problems. Even minor ones blacken the thoughts. But then the sun starts its climb in the east, pushing back night's darkness with its rosy fingers. And suddenly all looks brighter.

Such is the second picture Malachi presents— but more vividly. Over a world groping around in sin's darkness, grasping blindly at any straw, gazing fearfully at God's judgment, he saw the "sun of righteousness" rising. Might we not even spell it the "*Son* of righteousness," because that's whom Malachi meant? Not only would that coming Savior be totally righteous himself in person and actions, but he would bring total righteousness for a sinful world. His perfect sacrifice would cancel out all our unrighteous thoughts, words, and actions. And where there had been sin's darkness, there would now be light—light such as the world had never seen.

Just as the sun brings relief for aching bones, this Son would bring relief for aching hearts. Ask the believer whose conscience has been scarred and scared by sins what the Son's promise, "Go in peace, your sins are forgiven," means (Matthew 9:2). Ask the believer who feels all alone, orphaned in the surging sea of humanity, what the Son's promise, "Surely I will be with you always," means (Matthew 28:20). Ask the believer who, this holiday season, even more sorely misses that loved one lying under that cemetery's mound what the Son's promise, "He who believes in me will live, even though he dies," means (John 11:25). Ask those believers. Ask yourself. And we'll hardly need the Advent advice to stand in the Son-shine.

For the coming of the Son of righteousness into the manger and on the Last Day, Malachi waited and watched. Because of his coming, we rejoice and celebrate.

The King shall come when morning dawns and light and beauty brings. Hail, Christ the Lord! Your people pray: Come quickly, King of kings! Amen. (CW 25:5)

**11
DEC**

So John came, baptizing in the desert region and preaching a baptism of repentance for the forgiveness of sins. (Mark 1:4)

WE'RE LISTENING, JOHN

Little Megan was trying to tell me something. Home from the office, I had dropped into my chair and picked up the newspaper. Caught up in what I was doing, I didn't hear or see my granddaughter standing there. All at once her hand hit the paper and swatted it aside. "Grandpa, I'm talking to you," she announced.

This Advent season John the Baptist wants to talk to us, to speak to us about repentance. Each of us needs to hear what he has to say, for it has much to do with how we celebrate Christmas.

First of all, John speaks to us about our sins. To preach repentance means to preach sin—to describe it clearly and detail its consequences. John did that for those who came out into the wilderness to hear him. He stripped away their "everybody's doing it" alibi and showed their sin for what it really was: rebellion against God. He lifted the covers off their hearts and minds and dumped out the repulsive garbage of their sins right before their eyes and noses. He swabbed away the mist of respectability with which they had covered their lives and showed them for what they really were: lost and condemned sinners. Like a person on the tenth floor who crawls out onto a fireman's ladder once he's convinced the building is burning—so sinners need to see their desperate condition.

Several summers ago a family of skunks took up residence behind our garden shed and, looking for grubs, dug holes in our lawn. Every morning we could smell them. And what an odor it was! Now those skunks were so used to it that they couldn't smell one another. Somewhat similarly, the world around us is conditioned to sin—living in it, making excuses for it, overlooking it, even rolling around in it. Living in a world where sin abounds, we're always in danger of getting used to sin's smell. Advent is a time to clean out our nostrils and clear up the smell. Advent is a time to tune in to John the Baptist's message of repentance and realize he's also talking to us. Advent is a time to respond, "We're listening, John."

Second, John speaks to us about forgiveness. To preach repentance means to preach not only about sin's malady but also about sin's remedy. John also did that for those who went out to hear him in the wilderness. He even had the privilege of pointing his finger directly at the Lamb of God, who had come to take away the sins of the world and to baptize many for the forgiveness of sins. No wonder so many crowded around him. He offered what they needed.

Our world, like some stubborn child, often just closes its eyes and plows persistently ahead in its own stubborn and foolish furrow. It seeks solutions to its problems in itself rather than in the Lamb of God. To change people, to make them better, the world has tried civilization, education, legislation. Yet people continue to pillage and pilfer, hurt and harm—and with ever-increasing intensity. And they continue to despair, to die, and go to their eternal doom. So our 21st-century world needs to hear the message about the way back to the Father's house and to freedom from Satan, sin, and self through the Savior, cradled at Bethlehem and crucified on Calvary—just as the 1st-century world of John's day needed that message.

Let the world answer for itself. What's our answer to the Advent message? Better still, what's *my* answer? Is it "Speak to *me*, John, *I'm* listening. Tell me again why God came to our ball of mud. Why he took on my flesh. Why he went to that cross. Why he was plunged into the depths of hell. Why he rose from the grave. Tell me that it was *for me*. Tell me that because of him I am cleansed from every stain of sin, clothed with his righteousness, capable of living *for him* on earth and *with him* in heaven."

John preached this message the first Advent season. Now it's preached again to us. God open our ears to hear as we wait and watch for our Savior's second coming.

Oh, grant, dear Lord of love, that we receive, rejoicing, the word proclaimed by John, our true repentance voicing, that gladly we may walk upon our Savior's way until we live with him in his eternal day. Amen. (CW 20:4)

*I have been reminded of your sincere faith,
which first lived in your grandmother Lois and in
your mother Eunice and, I am persuaded, now lives
in you also. (2 Timothy 1:5)*

A FAMILY CHRISTMAS

Ever imagine that Jesus had a grandpa? One who
took him fishing or told him tales about his
famous ancestor King David? Or how about a
grandma? One who baked him cookies or let him
lick the mixing spoon? How about cousins who
played games with him? Could it be that they all
celebrated his birthday with him?

Christmas is family time. It's time to gather
from wherever family members live and to celebrate together. And if they can't get together, then
it's time for packages to go back and forth in the
mail with the presents that couldn't be hand
delivered and time for long-distance phone calls.
There's no generation gap at Christmastime.
Parents and grandparents say "Christmas is for
kids"—but they still appreciate the excitement
and treasure the meaning. The younger ones

learn the family traditions and join in the celebration. A baby's birth has brought them together. Believing families gather and rejoice because of the holy child of Bethlehem. The older generation learned it from the previous, the upcoming generation from the current—just as young Timothy learned about the Savior from his mother and grandmother.

In fact, the Christmas family is even wider. It embraces all those who, like Timothy, by God's grace, have faith in the babe of Bethlehem. Through Jesus the Savior, we are brothers and sisters, members of an even more wonderful family than our earthly one. Through him we share the privilege of having our names written in God's family register and of having a room reserved for us in his home.

Christmas is family time. Even as we gather to celebrate, we also remember. Perhaps more than any other time of the year, we think of loved ones who are gone. And we miss them. Now whether Timothy's grandmother was still alive when Paul wrote, we don't know. But she certainly must have had a spot in Timothy's heart, for she had helped pass the faith on to him. And because she had, Timothy knew even more about another joyous Christmas celebration—the heavenly one where hearts are perfect, songs of praise are pure, and true family members are present. Both appreciation for the past and anticipation of the future are part of the family Christmas celebration.

Christmas is family time. The new boyfriend or girlfriend—possible life partners—are looked over and look over the family circle. The new babies are handled and heralded by well-meaning aunts and touched with approval by loving uncles. And as each happy Christmas rolls around, the family circle grows wider and wider. The day could well be coming when Grandma won't be able to prepare a meal for all of them and when her modest house won't hold all of them.

What a picture of God's family! God's grace reaches across the seven continents and down through all the centuries. His gift of the babe of Bethlehem is for all the children of men. His family is composed of people of all colors, countries, and cultures. His home has room for them all. On earth they celebrate Christmas in different ways. In heaven their song will be the same. Eternity will echo with their joyous hymn, "Salvation belongs to our God, who sits on the throne, and to the Lamb" (Revelation 7:10).

Timothy spent his life working to widen God's family circle. He passed on to others what his mother and his grandmother and his mentor Paul had taught him. We can't all be missionaries like Timothy, but we can share the real meaning of Christmas. In our own way, in our own stations of life, we can help deliver our Father's Christmas gift to others.

As we celebrate, we wait and watch for our Savior's coming to carry us home. We also work so that others may wait and watch with us.

Oh, may he soon to ev'ry nation find entrance where he is unknown, with life and light and free salvation, that Satan's pow'r be overthrown, and healing to all hearts may come in heathen land and Christian home! Amen. (CW 32:5)

13 DEC

His father Zechariah was filled with the Holy Spirit and prophesied: "Praise be to the Lord, the God of Israel, because he has come and has redeemed his people." (Luke 1:67)

THAT'S OUR SONG

"That's our song." When my wife and I were dating, one song in particular meant a great deal to us. Every time we heard it on the radio, the look we gave each other said, "That's our song."

Zechariah, the father of John the Baptist, could have called his inspired prophecy about the Savior and his son John "My Song." His wife, Elizabeth, who shared his faith, might have added in agreement "Our Song." Hopefully all of us would be able to agree that his words are "our song" too.

As the aged priest held his eight-day-old son in his arms, he just had to sing. For in the birth of John, who was to prepare the way for the Savior, Zechariah—filled with the Holy Spirit—saw the certainty of Christ's birth. And while that wondrous event still lay sixth months in the future, Zechariah sang of it as if it had already happened.

"The Lord, the God of Israel . . . has come and has redeemed his people," he proclaimed for all to hear. The centuries of waiting and watching were over. Now it was time for unwrapping and for wondering in awe at God's gift.

Do we want to make Zechariah's song our own? Then, like him, we need to marvel at the miracle behind Bethlehem. He hadn't seen the Christ Child yet, but he knew who that baby would be. "The Lord, the God of Israel," he stated. In that coming child, he saw "God of God, Light of Light, Very God of Very God," as we also see and confess in the Nicene Creed (*The Lutheran Hymnal* [TLH]). Zechariah could understand the miracle behind that birth no more than we could, but, like us, he could marvel at the love involved.

Some time ago an article on space travel pointed out some impossible figures. A spaceship traveling 50,000 miles an hour would need hundreds of years to reach some of the stars. Any crew on board would be dead long before the spaceship reached such destinations. So their flight would become an impossible mission.

Yet our Lord did the impossible—he came down from the unreachable, with a love that is unmatchable, so that you and I might live forever with him in heaven. As we unwrap God's Christmas gift, let's never forget the miracle that was needed to achieve it and the love that provided it.

Zechariah sang that day not only because he saw who that holy child would be but also because he saw what that child would do. Again, inspired by the Spirit, he spoke as if it had already happened: "The Lord has redeemed his people."

Over the summer I read an interesting book about the winners of the Congressional Medal of Honor. One account particularly stuck in my mind—that of Master Sergeant Travis Watkins of Gladwater, Texas. On September 3, 1950, he was severely wounded by enemy gunfire near Yongsan, Korea. Though paralyzed from the waist down, he ordered his squad to pull out. He stayed behind and was killed covering their retreat. For that heroic deed, Congress posthumously granted him our country's highest medal.

The Lord came not to cover our retreat but to cover our sins. He came to free sinners—sinners already held captive and imprisoned by the enemy—and to claim them as soldiers of his cross and heirs of his heaven. His deeds required of him more than incredible bravery. They required unbelievable love. For his act of redemption, he deserves more than medals from us. He has earned our ongoing praise.

Advent is time again for each of us to look into the mirror and ask some serious questions: "Am I a sinner? How much, not how little, have I sinned? What do I deserve because of those sins? What would death be like without our Savior and Redeemer?" When we ask and answer such questions candidly, we'll reach for God's Christmas present and unwrap it with wonder. And we'll be more than ready to make Zechariah's song "our song."

Gracious Lord, we cannot thank and praise you enough for the miracle of love behind your birth and our redemption. Help us sing our songs of praise to you all our days. Amen.

14 DEC

Mary said: "My soul glorifies the Lord and my spirit rejoices in God my Savior." (Luke 1:46)

WHAT ARE WE GETTING FROM CHRISTMAS?

Only ten days left till Christmas Eve. Are you an impatient person—the kind that goes snooping in the family's usual hiding places or shakes the packages under the tree? Are you a curious person—the kind who's always wondering "What am I getting this Christmas?" If so, there's a much better question you might well ask as you continue your Advent and Christmas preparations: What am I getting *from* Christmas? Mary, the mother of Jesus, gives you an answer.

Did you ever wonder what it was like that day? Did you ever ask yourself how much noise do angels make in flight? Do they break the sound barrier? With what kind of voice do they talk? How do they, God's foremost invisible creatures, feel when they stand before sinful human beings? Much more important is this question: How would you have felt if you had been in Mary's shoes and the angel Gabriel were talking to you?

Fearful? It's no fun to be an unwed mother—in spite of modern society's trends. No fun to face the gossip of the community. No fun to be the topic of conversation out at the village well. No fun to think about the reaction of Joseph, your intended. What would he think? Even more important, what would he do? How difficult would it be to live without him and his love? And what about the law that stipulated that an adulteress should be stoned to death? You see, to consent to being an unwed mother, as the angel asked Mary to do, was not all that simple. If you had been there in her place, might you have been afraid too?

Yet it was not fear that moved Mary to hurry and visit her friend Elizabeth and to share the good news with her. Did you catch Mary's joyful tone? "My soul glorifies the Lord," she exclaimed. She began by praising her gracious God. Notice that Mary never pointed a finger at herself and asked to be praised. She sought no "Hail, Mary." She wanted all praise to go to the Lord. She wanted every alleluia and every hymn and every prayer to be directed to the One who had done such great things for her. And the greatest of all those things was his keeping his promise and sending the Savior.

Again, did you catch those most meaningful words? "My spirit rejoices in God my Savior," she sang. It wasn't *the* Savior but *my* Savior. This baby, planted by the Holy Spirit in Mary's womb and growing under her heart, was her Savior.

This baby, whom she would bring into the world with all the pains and dangers childbirth involves and whom she would swaddle in poor people's diapers, would be her Savior. This baby, whom she would watch grow in strength and size and under whose cross she would shudder, was her Savior. Mary, by God's grace and working, knew what she was getting *from* that first Christmas. It was the Savior—not only the world's but also hers.

Ever watch little ones unwrapping Christmas presents? They don't care about breaking ribbons or preserving paper. They just want to get at the present inside, so they go at it with gusto. How about our unwrapping of the present we receive from God every Christmas? Someone once wrote: "To say that Christ was born is history. To say that Christ was born to save sinners is theology. To say that Christ was born to save me, the sinner—that's salvation." You and I, by the grace of God, can repeat those most glorious words.

So let's go at our gifts from Christmas. But let's do more than size up this year's packages in anticipation or shake them in curiosity. Let's go back into those early chapters of the gospels and read again how the wondrous gift was given. Let's use the special services as joyful, thankful times in which to unwrap and wonder at the Savior each one of us has received from our loving Father.

Gracious Father, gifts belong with Christmas. Help us remember that our giving to our loved ones is but a faint reflection of what you have given to us. Cause the birth of Jesus my Savior to be at the heart of my Christmas joy. Amen.

15
DEC

When Joseph woke up, he did what the angel of the Lord had commanded him and took Mary home as his wife. But he had no union with her until she gave birth to a son. And he gave him the name Jesus. (Matthew 1:24,25)

BUILDING UP FAITH'S MUSCLES

We finally have gotten rid of our son's stuff. All through graduate school and several moves to different states, his boxes of stuff stood lined up against our basement wall. When he finally settled, we started moving those boxes, one carload at a time. On one particular trip, as I shoehorned his bench and weights into the car, memories came flooding back. The picture of him as a teenager, lifting those weights and working out day after day to build up his muscles, flashed before my mind.

Faith's muscles always need work. Building up faith's strength comes not from a regular regimen of lifting weights but from listening to God's Word. Such is the Advent truth we learn from Joseph, the stepfather of the Savior.

Joseph had his share of problems the night the angel came to see him. He had the same dreams as many of us have—dreams of getting married, settling down, starting a family. But those dreams had received a kick in the teeth. His bride-to-be was pregnant—and not by him. Can you imagine his anxious thoughts as he worked in the carpenter shop, walked the streets of Nazareth, or lay awake on his bed? What should he do? If he accused Mary of adultery, the penalty for her would be severe. He loved her too much for that, even if she had hurt him. He finally reached the anguished conclusion that the best thing he could do for her would be to give her up, put her away quietly, and live without her—the one he loved. Already at that point, Joseph revealed his strength of faith. He wanted to do what was right in the sight of God and best for his betrothed. He was motivated by love.

We see Joseph's strength of faith even more clearly in his reaction after the angel came to see him that night. What a message that angel had for him—one about a virgin birth, a child whose name had already been picked, and a vital mission for a lost world. No, Joseph couldn't understand how a baby could be virgin born or how God could become man. But he believed those promises. And his faith was as much God's miracle as the special birth of that baby was.

With the strength of faith God gave him, Joseph obeyed the angel and took Mary as his wife. With the strength of faith, he loved her and cared for her, and in due time she gave birth to his and the world's Savior. With the strength of faith, he gave his stepson the name chosen in heaven—Jesus. With the strength of faith, he obeyed God's command and took mother and child to safety in Egypt. With the strength of faith, he led his family to Nazareth, where he made a home for them and provided for them. Some 12 years later, this man of faith disappeared from the scene, and Scripture says no more about him. But what it does say is enough for us to want a faith like his.

Do we need to build up faith's muscles? Or are they strong enough? How truthful should we be about this? How honest should we be about the umpteen times our faith stumbled instead of believing God's promises? About confessing how our faith stubbed its toe instead of striding forward in Christian response? Many of us are painfully aware of the frequent "yes, but" excuse we give to our God. He tells us of his presence and pardon, his providence and protection—and all we can do is hesitate and stammer. He asks us to love our spouses and family members, our neighbors and fellow world dwellers—and the best we can do is act in spurts and make excuses for our failures.

Time to pray again this Advent season: "Lord, give us strength for our faith." As we do, it's time to remember again where Joseph found strength for his faith—in the gracious promises of God.

The more we lift those promises daily, the more his Spirit will build up the muscles of our faith.

Lord, we believe; help our unbelief. Help us unwrap your gospel promises regularly and wonder at what they tell us. Build up our faith so that, with Joseph, we can name that baby "Jesus" and, in him, find pardon for our sins and power for our lives. Amen.

16 DEC

Suddenly a great company of the heavenly host appeared with the angel, praising God and saying, "Glory to God in the highest, and on earth peace to men on whom his favor rests." (Luke 2:13,14)

FRONT ROW SEATS

Front row seats—that's what a colleague and I had in New York City. In town to attend a seminar, we stopped at a theater box office window. We didn't really expect to get tickets for the first line play. We just thought we'd give it a try. Imagine our surprise when the ticket agent offered us two seats in the front row. Did we take them? You bet! And we thoroughly enjoyed the show.

No man-made production, however, could ever come close to matching God's presentation in the sky over Bethlehem that first Christmas. And look, just look, at who was sitting in those front row seats.

Don't you wish you could have heard God's angels sing in that heaven-cast show? Did they sing in four-part harmony? Were there soloists? And what did they look like, those angels who formed that heavenly chorus? To whom did they sing? Who sat in the front row? No princes or priests, no kings or ambassadors, not even the Roman emperor sat in those front row seats. Just shepherds, common shepherds, were in attendance for this premier performance. To the commonest of the common, to the crustiest of the undercrust—God sent his angelic chorus to deliver the greatest message ever heard.

"Why?" we ask. The answer lies in the fact that humble shepherds fit right in with God's choice of a humble village named Bethlehem and a humble mother named Mary. In emphasizing such details, the heavenly author of the Christmas story is making a most important point: When it comes to Bethlehem and when it comes to Calvary—where salvation and heaven are involved—anyone and everyone can have a front row seat. In fact, there are only front row seats. And they are reserved for all, regardless of their earthly state, station, or stature. No one is excluded. The Savior was born, died, and rose again for one and *for all*—including *you* and *me*.

More important than the question, Why to shepherds? is the answer to the question, What did the angels tell those shepherds? "On earth peace," they said. Sin had ripped out of Adam and Eve's grasp the peace God had given them. Since that rueful day, a holy God's words, "There is no peace to the wicked," struck cold terror into every sinner's heart. Regardless of where they looked on earth, there was no peace to be found, that is, until that night at Bethlehem. Looking down on the Christ Child, the angels had to sing. In the Christ Child, they beheld the Prince of peace. In the Christ Child, they saw the means God would use to reestablish peace between himself and man—Christ's suffering and death on the cross, which paid for mankind's sins. So the angels used that word *peace* to sum up the meaning of the Christ Child's birth—a message intended not only for those shepherds but for all mankind.

"On earth peace," those angels sang. But we might answer: "Where? You call what I have in my life right now peace? What about those sins that come back to haunt me? What about those sins into which I fall each day and which never seem to go away? What about peace for all that?" Remember what the shepherds did with the angels' message of peace? They hurried to the manger and knelt before the Prince of peace. Only when we join them in unwrapping God's Christmas gift and wondering in awe at this most precious and holy gift will we find peace for our sins.

What about that loss of a loved one? You call those bruises on the heart, sobs in the soul, emptiness in the home, peace? Again, let's remember what the shepherds did. Let's rise from kneeling at our loved ones' graves and hurry to Bethlehem to unwrap and wonder at God's Christmas gift. There in the manger lies the

Prince of peace and Lord of life, who turns sorrow into joy and death into victory.

What about problems with my spouse or drifting child? What about those inner fears and frustrations that inhabit my heart? What about my broken dreams and cloudy future? By now we should know the answer. We must hurry with the shepherds to the manger bed of the One who even now offers peace in the midst of the very real problems of life.

Front row seats—that's what our gracious God has given us. From those seats we can see close up what his Christmas gift is all about. Let our unwrapping and joyful wondering begin and never cease.

Thank you, Lord, for putting us in the front row of Christmas. Fill our hearts with the peace of Christmas and the joy of our salvation. Amen.

17 DEC

This is love: not that we loved God, but that he loved us and sent his Son as an atoning sacrifice for our sins. Dear friends, since God so loved us, we also ought to love one another. (1 John 4:10,11)

LOVE'S PURE LIGHT

Funny what the ears of little children hear. Though my wife had taught her class the passage "he careth for you" (1 Peter 5:7 KJV) as memory work, one first grader recited, "Eat carrots for you." That's what that little student had heard. I had a similar "hearing" problem. As a child, it took me some time before I realized that the hymn "Silent Night" didn't read "Son of God, love's *poor* light" but "Son of God, love's *pure* light."

There's nothing poor about the love we behold in Bethlehem's manger. From the world, we expect a love that is self-serving and self-seeking—only looking for what it can get out of it. Or a love that is self-rewarding—reaching out only to those who have done or will do something in return. Or a love that's fickle—that flickers with each shifting wind. The world's type of love would never in a million years have put the Christ Child into that manger. Only God's love could and would. In the babe of Bethlehem, birthed in a stable and bedded in a manger, we see love's true light.

The word John used for love is unique. It refers to a love that goes out to the unlovable, a love that is totally undeserved. We might even say that it is a love that loves—not because of but in spite of what we are. Such love is divine. It is unique to God. Only God can love the unlovable and give to the undeserving. "God is love," we learned in our Sunday school days. Only from him whose very essence is love can pure love come.

Now look at the manger. See how real God's love is. It's not just talk with no action. See also how far his love is willing to go. What would bring a God who dwells in magnificent splendor into a scratchy straw-filled manger? What would bring him to a hill with a bloodstained cross? And what would bring him to a tomb as a bloodstained corpse.

Notice also to whom God's love goes. "Us," John wrote. And we are painfully aware of what kind of "us" we are. How could God love people like us—people who did not, could not, would not love him? How could God love people like us—people whose sinful hearts made us his antagonists and whose sinful lives were spent in action against him?

"He loves me," little Kathy whispered, as she slid closer to her mother in the church bench and squeezed the Sunday school leaflet with Jesus' picture on it. For her the message was clear: "Jesus loves me." For us too as we kneel before the manger bed of God. There in the Son of God is love's pure light.

What are we to do with such love? Unwrap it and wonder at it? Of course! But that's not all. Keep it going. Give it back. Love in response. So, husbands and wives, show his love—not just at Christmas and on anniversaries but repeatedly. Children and parents of all ages, show his love— not just periodically or haphazardly but regularly. Church members of different backgrounds, ages, and professions show his love—not just to your own kind but to all. Neighbors, show his love to those who live next door to you and down the block. Pick one person a month to show a little more love to, and not just the most agreeable person you can find either. And what is the best way yet to show love to anyone? Tell them how God put his own Son in that Bethlehem manger as "love's pure light."

When I visited children in the hospital, I would often give them a glow-in-the-dark memento of Jesus and the children. In the middle of the night, they could look at Jesus and see him holding little children, like them, and be comforted. But that memento would glow only after it had been exposed to real light. And so it is with our response to God's love. The "poor light" of our reflecting love grows only as it is exposed again and again to the "pure light" of God's love in Christ.

Good reason, wouldn't you say, for us to unwrap and wonder frequently at God's Christmas gift of love?

What a gift of love you placed into that manger, Lord. Help us to treasure what your love has given us in Jesus and to shine with your love to those around us. Amen.

18 DEC

I am the light of the world. Whoever follows me will never walk in darkness, but will have the light of life. (John 8:12)

CAN YOU SEE THE LIGHT?

When I first met Arnie in the nursing home, he was blind. Years of an excessive lifestyle had cost him his profession, his wife, his family, and finally his eyesight. When I visited his roommate, who was one of our members, I would make sure to speak loudly enough so that Arnie might also hear the gospel. One day, after months of such visits, Arnie motioned me over to his bedside. "What do I have to do to join your church?" he asked. And it went forward from there. Three months later on his deathbed, he said, "Thank God I can see Jesus." "What shall I preach at your funeral?" I asked. "Tell them to see Jesus, the light" was his answer.

Christmas and light go together. Lights on the rooflines of our houses and on the trees in our bay windows. Lights arching over our streets and looped in and around our outdoor displays. What would Christmas be without lights? More important, what would Christmas be for us without Jesus, the Light of the world? Can we, do we, see the light this Christmas?

"I am the light of the world," Jesus said. For good reason. Think of how pure and untarnished light is in this world. Man's grubby hands can't dirty its rays. Earth's pollution can't defile its beams. It's the same with Jesus, the Light of the world. He took on the sins of the world but never knew sin's stain. In Bethlehem's manger he was the holy child. In his walk through life, he felt temptation, yet he remained the spotless Lamb of God. Compared to him "not so brightly beameth the sun in yonder skies," as we sing in one of our Christmas hymns.

We don't need to put spotlights on the manger in our Christmas crèche. The sinless Light of the world lies in that cradle. Can we, do we, see him as we unwrap and wonder at the miracle of it all this season?

Could we marvel at a sunset if there were no light? Or take pictures of mountain scenes with our cameras if clouds covered them? Light brings brightness. What a picture of Jesus, the Light of the world. Without him the world grovels in darkness, groping blindly around for any glimmer of hope— and finding none! Without him only a life full of problems, a grave full of death, and a hell full of suffering lie ahead. To those who are sitting in the shadow of unbelief and speeding toward outer darkness, Jesus came as the light of salvation.

There simply is no brightness of salvation without him. Only that soul is bright which has Jesus in it. Only that page is bright on which Christ is found. Only that worship service is bright in which Christ is worshiped. Only that Christmas is bright which is built around Jesus, the light of heaven, the Morning Star.

Without light there is no life. Ever try growing tomato plants in a windowless basement? Or start bedding plants in a closet? It doesn't work. It takes the sun's warmth to swell the seeds in the pots and the buds on the trees. So with Christ. Where he is not present with his light, there can be only spiritual dreariness and desolation. But where his beams shine forth through Word and sacrament, dead hearts are brought to faith and barren lives bloom with fruit. And those hearts are being readied for heaven's eternal life as he continues to shine in them.

One of my favorite verses about heaven describes it as a city that "does not need the sun or the moon to shine on it, for the glory of God gives it light, and the Lamb is its lamp" (Revelation 21:23). Don't you look forward a bit more eagerly each Christmas to seeing that heavenly light? God help us remember Arnie's words. God help us unwrap and wonder anew at the gift of Jesus, the Light, every day.

Lord, you have opened our eyes and shown us the brightness of your salvation in Christ Jesus. Draw us more and more into your gospel so that our faith grows and brings forth fruit for you. Keep our eyes on Jesus till, in heaven, we see him as the Light of the world in all his brightness. Amen.

I have come that they may have life, and have it to the full. (John 10:10)

GET A LIFE!

"Get a life!" I heard the clerk say under her breath as the complaining customer finally turned away. The clerk's mistake—packing the man's groceries in a plastic bag instead of a paper sack—had resulted in a vociferous complaint from the customer. Though the clerk received the rebuke submissively, she couldn't resist responding, "Get a life." And she was right. There are more important things to get excited about than paper sacks or plastic bags for our groceries.

Christmas and excitement go together. It is exciting to pick out and put up a tree. To plan and purchase suitable gifts. To prepare and find pleasure in family gatherings and dinners. But "get a life!" There are far more important things—like the Christ Child in the manger with his gift of real life for sinners like us.

Life came into the manger that first Christmas. Not just a living, breathing, new baby boy but life to the full. Not just the miracle of an eternal God now living in human flesh—but the special life he came to bring. The world constantly probes and prods at the thing it calls life. It experiments with embryonic transplants and cloning cells in order to initiate life. It researches, avidly looking for modern fountains of youth in order to lengthen life. It frequently changes its definition of life's end from "no more breath" to "no more pulse" and, even more recently, to "no more brain waves." Yet, when all is said and done, the world still has to scratch its head and admit its inadequacy in controlling what it calls life.

If only the world would realize its inadequacy when it comes to real life. Ever since the fall into sin in Eden's garden, every baby has been born spiritually dead. Its inheritance from its sinful parents is a heart that is full of unbelief, and that can lead only to a life filled with sinful thoughts, words, and actions. Dead in sin and doomed to eternal damnation, the sinner can do nothing to change his condition. In fact, he doesn't want to. And when the message of salvation comes his way, his only response is to punch it aside as foolishness. Not only is his condition mortal, but it's fatal. Yet he walks, sometimes even struts, around as if he were really living.

This advent we take time, we make time, to kneel at the manger of One who brings us life. "He who has the Son has life; he who does not have the Son of God does not have life," John stated so clearly (1 John 5:12). We know, by God's grace, what we have in that newly born baby in the manger. "Jesus gives us life without the big 'if' in the middle" is the way someone once put it. From Jesus, then, comes a life that no longer fears but trusts God. A life that no longer is bogged down under sin's weight but flies high through forgiveness. A life that no longer revels in sin but rejoices in doing God's will. A life that no longer is shuffling off relentlessly on the way to hell but has heaven's ticket in its hand.

Do we need someone to tell us to "get a life" before we realize what we really ought to be excited about this Christmas? Or can we answer, "I've got a life—a wonderful, beautiful life in Jesus," and that's why we're so excited.

Just imagine how even more excited we'll be when the eternal Christmas comes. Don't blow out the candles on Jesus' birthday cake. The best is yet to come. What "life to the full" will be ours in heaven, where all sin, temptation to sin, and results of sin are completely gone. What "life to the full" will be ours when our mortal bodies put on immortality and are rejoined with our souls for a forever existence. What ceaseless unwrapping and wondering will be ours as we experience the perfect life God will give us.

Little children can hardly wait for Christmas to come. God's children are even more excited about the eternal Christmas that is coming. And all because they "got a life" through God's gift of life in the manger.

Gracious Lord, thank you for sending your Son to bring us life. Keep us alive in him all our days, and take us to live with him in the glories of heaven. Amen.

Peace I leave with you; my peace I give you. I do not give to you as the world gives. Do not let your hearts be troubled and do not be afraid. (John 14:27)

A PIECE OF THAT PEACE

"I'd sure like a piece of that peace," said the beleaguered husband in my study. He was there to seek advice on a serious marriage situation. Both he and his wife had drifted in their relationship with their Lord, and the results were showing up in the troubles they were experiencing with each other. When I pointed him back to the peace Christ brings, he blurted out the words above.

Peace is not something with which our world is well supplied. Our world lives and breathes conflict, as the news media testifies nearly every day. Is it much different with us in our individual lives? How many of us are at war with ourselves over something we've done in the past, are involved in right now, or are contemplating for the future? Would any of us care to peel off the layers that hide hearts from view and reveal the turmoil going on there? How many of us, like that beleaguered husband, are at war with someone else, even someone close to us? Wars without and wars within—that seems to be an accurate picture of the world we live in and the individual lives we lead.

Why? Why is it that way? The answer is amazingly simple and spelled out in one word—*sin*. Conflict is caused by sin, and that sin resides in our hearts. There, for example, we find the peace masher called selfishness. A selfish person can never be a peaceful person. Let no one dare to advance above him, gain more than he has, have brighter ideas than his. He must be first. And such striving invariably leads to conflict. The second peace masher is revenge. Let his dignity be wounded, his path crossed, his plans spoiled, and revenge starts burning in his heart. And it burns even fiercer as he schemes how to get even. The third peace masher is envy. Shakespeare called it "the green sickness." Envy sold Joseph into slavery, drove David into adultery, threw Daniel into the lion's den, and put Jesus on trial. Where envy lurks, people roll up their sleeves, ready to quarrel and begrudging others almost anything.

Do we know people like this? Even more seriously—am I ever like this? Would I rather push ahead than back down? Hit back or hit first rather than turn the other cheek? Get even, rather than patch things up? Serious questions and honest answers show us how we have wrapped layer after layer and tied knot upon knot of sin around God's precious gift of peace.

"Half of knowledge is to know where to find knowledge" reads the inscription over the graduate school hall entrance at Florida State University in Tallahassee. Over the entrance to the stable at Bethlehem, we might write a similar inscription: "Half of peace is to know where to find peace." "Prince of Peace" the prophet Isaiah called that baby. "Peace on earth," the angels sang at his birth. "Peace," the Savior himself promised all his disciples on the way to the cross—a peace unlike any that the world could ever offer.

For us, peace is found—not in summit meetings with endless talk about the limitation and elimination of nuclear weapons. Nor in extensive seminars that seek to analyze and program the human being. But in Jesus! "My peace," Jesus himself calls it—a peace he came to prepare. A peace that only God could give. His manger bed was the first step on his way to the cross, and there he removed the sin that set all mankind at horrible odds with a holy God.

Not only did he prepare this heavenly peace, but he also portrayed it. Do we want an example of how those who have peace with God react toward their fellowman? Then look at Jesus. He lived peace, modeling and championing it all his earthly days. From the one flows the other. At peace with God, sinners strive to live more at peace with one another.

This season, as we unwrap and wonder at God's gift of peace in the manger, let our prayer be, "Lord, give us not just a piece of peace with you but all of it." And then let our prayer continue, "Lord, give us an increasing piece of the resulting peace with our fellowmen."

How wonderful it is, Lord, that we can talk to you! Thank you for sending your Son to give us peace with you by removing the barrier of our sin. Help us treasure that peace and live in it with our fellowmen. Amen.

21 DEC

The Word became flesh and made his dwelling among us. We have seen his glory, the glory of the One and Only, who came from the Father, full of grace and truth. (John 1:14)

A WORD WE CAN SEE

"Are you there, Daddy?" asked little Sam. "Yes, Sam, I'm right over here," answered his father as they settled down for the night in their motel room beds. "But, Daddy, I don't just want to hear you. I want to see you too," said Sam a few minutes later. So his father got up, turned on the light in the bathroom, and left the door ajar. Then Sam went to sleep, content that he could now see his father's face.

What does God look like? Haven't you ever wondered? Or wanted to see him? Then come along to the Bethlehem manger. There lies the Word become flesh. We're so used to using the term *word* for sounds that come out of our mouths. John uses it to denote a person—God himself, come down from heaven and into our flesh as the living Word. We're so used to using "words" to reveal what's on our hearts and in our minds. John uses the term *word* for Jesus—a Word in whom we can both see and hear God. In Jesus, the eternal, invisible God graciously stepped into our world to reveal himself to us. In short, to see Jesus is to see God. And to hear Jesus is to hear God. "God in focus," we might call Jesus. The Savior himself made it perfectly clear when he said, "Anyone who has seen me has seen the Father" (John 14:9).

Do we sometimes downsize Christmas, shrinking it to infant size? Neither God nor Christmas is small. *Incredible, immense, indescribable* are words that fit much better. Look in the manger. There lies the Word—Jesus Christ, who has always been and is always the same yesterday, today, and forever. He who has always been one with the Father now lives among us. The Word is flesh and blood, alive and breathing—come to show us the Father. Here's the miracle above all miracles: a Word we can both hear and see.

An old Greek proverb states, "A word is the image of the soul." Just as we use words to show others what's in our hearts, so God showed us his heart by sending his Son into the manger. And what does the living Word show us about the Father's heart? It's a heart "full of grace and truth." It's a heart that will do anything to save lost mankind. It's a heart that would much rather welcome people to heaven than consign them to hell. It's a heart that yearns for his prodigal sons and daughters and will give the best he has to get them back. It's a heart that even took that impossible step across the unbridgeable gap between his holy heaven and our sinful world to beat in a human chest at Bethlehem and stop beating on an inhumane cross at Calvary. What do we see when we look at Jesus, the living Word? "God is love" is the answer—love beyond belief. That gigantic, awesome love we unwrap and wonder at this Advent season.

Remember lifeboat 14 from the "unsinkable" ship *Titanic?* After an iceberg tore a 300-foot gash in the *Titanic's* starboard side, it took 2 hours and 40 minutes for the ship to go under. During that time 20 lifeboats were launched. The survivors aboard them rowed away from the sinking ship as quickly as possible. They didn't want to be pulled down by the powerful undertow when the ship sank. After the *Titanic* went down, only lifeboat 14 went looking for survivors. All the others just paddled aimlessly around. They heard the cries of the people in the water, but they made no effort to help them. They were afraid that if they pulled more people into their boats, they might sink.

Those who have seen and heard God's saving heart in Jesus, the Word, don't remain on their knees at his manger bed. They get up and go to work. They realize that there are people out there in danger of drowning in their sin. They realize, with loving concern, that there's a world out there that still has not seen or heard the Word. They recognize, of course, that it's a big job to carry the gospel to every creature, but that doesn't stop them. For even more so do they recognize how big God's gift of the Word was that first Christmas.

To whom will I carry the message of Jesus this season? Whom can I help both hear and see this saving Word so they can get rid of their fear of the dark?

Thank you, Lord, for giving me eyes to see and ears to hear Jesus, the living message of your love for sinners like me. Help me bring this message to others, so they can join me kneeling in grateful joy before his manger bed. Amen.

We have put our hope in the living God, who is the Savior of all men, and especially of those who believe. (1 Timothy 4:10)

I HOPE SO? OR I KNOW SO!

"I hope so?" people sometimes say, raising their voices in question at the end. For them hope is often wishful thinking, a yearning for something to be true. But they aren't quite sure. So the question mark results.

Kneeling before God's Christmas gift, believers don't respond, "I hope so?" They don't question whether the Christ Child is what he says or whether he offers what he claims. For them "I hope so?" is really "I know so!" with an exclamation point. With eyes of faith, they see hope in person in the manger—God come to be their Savior. In this heaven-sent Savior, they confidently rest their own hopes for heaven.

Hope is important, no doubt about it. Remove hope from the human heart, and it becomes a broken heart—one that ceases its striving and sinks into despair. Hope often fails—no doubt about that statement either. Broken hopes litter the landscape of life and leave their owners bitterly disillusioned.

Hope's foundation is all important. Just as a house is only as solid as the concrete footings on which it rests, so hope is only as good as the foundation on which it rests. The foundation guarantees the reality of the thing hoped for.

The problem for many people is that they put whatever hope they have for eternity on the wrong foundation. Instead of trusting in the Christ Child, they rely on themselves. Instead of leaning on Christ's saving work, they rely on their own imperfect efforts. Instead of living in peaceful confidence, they squirm and sweat, especially when their end comes. Their hope's foundation proves to be a shallow crust over a sinkhole, through which they plunge into hell.

So what's our hope for eternity? There he is—in the manger. Rightly do we sing of the Christ Child, "The hopes and fears of all the years are met in thee tonight." Jesus is the only hope for a prodigal son and a penitent thief, a wayward woman and a Roman centurion, a blunt fisherman and a hesitant tax collector. Best of all, he's *our* only hope.

God came into our flesh to do what only God could do. Only the blood of the God-man could be precious enough to pay for our sins. Only his resurrection could be a safe guarantee that we too shall join him in his mansion in the skies. Only those who put their hope in him will not be ashamed.

What happens to a canoe that's not lashed to a tree on the shore? Have you ever made that mistake when camping? Either the water's motion carries it gradually out into the lake, or a storm's fierceness turns it into kindling.

Judas could tell us what happens to those who aren't tied to Christ. So also could David, Peter, and Paul. And so could you and I at various times in our lives. Faith is the rope that ties us to Christ, our hope. And that rope needs constant retying.

What better time than this special season to step up our personal Bible reading and to take advantage of those extra church services? Through the gospel the Spirit works to strengthen faith's ties to Jesus, our sure hope. Then let the storms of life come—the trials and troubles, the sins and sorrows, the dangers and difficulties. Those anchored to Christ are safe. Their Advent prayer fits: "Come, O precious Ransom, come, only Hope for sinful mortals!" (CW 8:1).

"I hope so?" or "I know so!" What will it be? Time to get busy unwrapping and wondering anew at God's grace in putting hope into the manger as our eternal gift.

Lord Jesus, thank you for coming into our world to be the only hope for sinful mortals. Keep our eyes of faith fastened on you as our only hope for heaven and our only help for this life. In your name we ask it. Amen.

Rejoice in the Lord always. I will say it again: Rejoice! (Philippians 4:4)

HAVE YOURSELF A MERRY *BIG* CHRISTMAS

"Have yourself a merry *little* Christmas," the song goes. And so often that's the problem, isn't it? Our Christmas is too little. It's far too small, too narrow, too confined. It doesn't last as long as it ought or do what it should. On this last Advent day before Christmas Eve, Paul urges us to have ourselves a merry *big* Christmas—one that lasts all year.

"Rejoice!" he commands. Why, we might ask. Don't we know how? Isn't that what our whole Christmas season is all about? There are the gifts and the gatherings. The fun that comes from watching children and grandchildren tear open presents that they hadn't even dreamed about getting. The feeling that warms the heart at having the family circle all gathered together. What joy to get together, share lives, catch up on news. What a shame that it so often waits until this time of the year to happen. So what do you mean by "Rejoice," Paul? We do, don't we?

Besides this, there are other things, you know. There's the job that, though I grumble about it at times, I'd be lost without. The spouse at my side, who, though I don't always appreciate enough, I surely wouldn't want to lose. The savings and investments—at least enough for a proverbial rainy day and a reasonable retirement. The vehicle or vehicles in the garage, the gadgets in the kitchen, the electronic gear in the family room, the extras I've become so accustomed to that I think I have to have them. So what do you mean, Paul, "Rejoice"? We do, don't we?

Be careful. These are only things and situations and circumstances. To center our joy on such items sets us up for a fall. For what happens to our joy when things are taken from us and circumstances change? How do I rejoice, then, when my bank account is heading for empty or a part of my body misbehaves? How do I rejoice, then, when a spouse deserts or a child disappoints? What's going to happen to such shallow joy when life no longer goes my way and circumstances no longer are colored rosy bright?

Paul was thinking of a *much bigger* Christmas when he wrote to the Christians at Philippi, "Rejoice in the Lord always." Remember where Paul was at the time—in a prison cell in Rome, locked up for the crime of talking about his Savior. Remember too what the usual mode of exit from a Roman prison cell was, even for a Roman citizen like Paul—as a corpse. If anything, we would have expected the apostle to be down and out, not speaking about rejoicing in the Lord always. What was his secret?

We don't have to guess. He tells us, "Rejoice *in the Lord.*" Paul's joy rose far above things and circumstances. It rested in the Lord. Paul's joy was great and unending, because he had a God who was great and unending. No prison door could shut his Savior out. No sorrow could steal away his joy, because his Savior could transform even such things into good. Even death could not sever him from his joy—it was the doorway to fuller joy at his Savior's side.

Do we want to have ourselves a merry *big* Christmas, one that outlasts the trees and the tinsel? Then, in the days ahead, let's go to Bethlehem and take our loved ones with us. Let's enter the stable where the Savior lies bedded on the hay and unwrap and wonder at the wondrous gift we have in him. Let's pick that baby up, cradle him in our hearts, and never put him down. And let's share the joy. There are so many who have only a five-cent joy when the five-million one is waiting for them in that baby in the manger. If we don't tell them, how will they ever join us in singing, "Joy, oh, joy beyond all gladness, Christ has done away with sadness"?

So how *big* is our merry Christmas going to be this year?

Lord, thank you for wrapping your Son in our flesh and sending him into our world of sin to be our Savior. Help us rejoice in his birth not just this season but all year through. Bring and keep us kneeling before the Savior's manger bed, that we may have ourselves a merry big Christmas. Amen.

He will be called Wonderful Counselor, Mighty God, Everlasting Father, Prince of Peace. (Isaiah 9:6)

IT'S TIME TO THINK ABOUT NAMES

"We don't even have a boy's name picked out," said my wife after giving birth to our second son. Somehow we had just assumed the baby would be a girl and had all kinds of appropriate names picked. But none for a boy. With that baby nestled in her arms, it was time for us to think about names.

The baby, at whose manger bed believers kneel this Christmas Eve, was named long before his birth. In fact, the prophet Isaiah, seven hundred years earlier, had picked a handful of names for this baby boy, and all of them were appropriate.

"Wonderful Counselor" was one name Isaiah picked. In those days too, a counselor was one who stood at someone's side to offer good advice in all matters. What an appropriate name for the Christ of Christmas. He is the Counselor, more wonderful than any other. He needs no teachers but is truth himself. His advice is never lacking and is always on the mark. To wayward ones he says, "Your sins are forgiven." To weary ones he says, "Cast all your cares on me for I care for you." To worried ones he says, "Will not my heavenly Father much more care for you?" To weeping ones he says, "Let not your heart be troubled; believe also in me."

The babe of Bethlehem, during his lifetime on earth, experienced our wrestling against sin and Satan, our pains and death, and even something we shall never know—the agonies of the damned in hell. He not only advises, but he also does. He did his work on the cross and now stands ready to help in every step of life as our loving Wonderful Counselor.

"Mighty God" was another name Isaiah gave him. Looking at the baby in the manger, we may fail to see in him the mighty God. That's God who is our rock and our fortress? Why, a rock could so easily crush him in his helplessness. That's God who is our shield and our defender? Why, he himself must be defended from harm and shielded from cold in his mother's arms. Yes, indeed! That baby is the mighty God who calms storms and heals men. Even more so do we see his might when he shouts of sin's payment on the cross: "It is finished." Even more so do we see his might when he leaves the grave empty and assures us, "Because I live, you also shall live." Yes, that humble baby is the mighty God, our loving Lord and Savior.

In his name "Everlasting Father," we see tender-ness, love, and comfort. To his followers the babe of Bethlehem is like a father because of what he does. He does not stand aloof from his people, leaving them to shift for themselves. Instead, he does for them what an earthly father can only try to do for his children. An earthly father tries to provide what he thinks is best; the Savior always provides what he knows is best. An earthly father tries to listen to his children; the Savior does listen, does understand, does solve our problems, if we but let him. An earthly father must, at last, leave his children; our Christ is an everlasting Father who guides his children through this vale of tears, even through the valley of the shadow to his home in heaven.

Isaiah's last name for the Savior is the best. "Prince of Peace" he called him. Not peace on earth, which is often fleeting and so quickly fractured, but peace with God this child offers. He brings the peace that floods the heart when man knows God is his dear friend and not his dreaded foe. The peace that comes when man knows that heaven is his beautiful home and hell is not his inevitable destination. From this Prince comes the peace that enables us to live in this tense world, that sustains us in moments of sorrow, and that equips us to face eternity unafraid. What a fitting name for this baby.

Tonight, as we kneel before his manger bed, it's time to give him a name. What better ones can we find than those Isaiah gave him? And what greater love can we find than God's love for sinners behind each of those names?

That love is what Christmas is all about.

Father in heaven, open our hearts to believe, our ears to hear, our eyes to see, our mouths to speak, our hands to share—that all may know the name of your Son, who was born that we might die to sin, and who died that we might live forever. Amen.

God so loved the world that he gave his one and only Son, that whoever believes in him shall not perish but have eternal life. (John 3:16)

OUR BEST CHRISTMAS GIFT

What's the best Christmas gift you ever received? That might be difficult to answer. Most of us have received so many over the years. Or would the answer be easy? It should be! There's one gift that's always the same, always the best—regardless of how many Christmases we've celebrated. And just why is it the best? Simple. It comes from our God, and it gives us just what we need.

Notice the tag on God's Christmas gift? "To the world," it says. Strange that God should give a gift to the world—for that world is made up of people who are God's enemies, people who are intent only on lashing out at him with their sins and hating him with their evil hearts. That world is made up of people who deserved nothing from him but the full hand of his anger and the full force of his punishment. To such people who had wronged him over and over again with their sins, God gave his Son as Savior.

Look once again at that tag on God's Christmas gift. Notice another name on it? "Whoever," it says, and that's you and me. Didn't the Christmas angel say the same thing? "Today in the town of David a Savior has been born," he announced, "to *you*." Today, across this world of ours, many are kneeling before the babe of Bethlehem and worshiping him as the Savior. But little good will come of our joining them unless we joyously say, "He's *my* Savior. He's my own personal, my best, Christmas gift."

We're all aware of the impractical Christmas gifts that fill our closets and eventually wind up on rummage sale tables. After all, what's a father to do with all those ties he receives Christmas after Christmas? Or just how many bottles of perfume can a wife or mother really use? Or how often haven't you told a person who just handed you a present, "You really shouldn't have," when you really meant, "I wish you hadn't." Impractical gifts, indeed.

Now let's take another look at God's Christmas gift to us? What could be more practical, more useful? Unlike some of the gifts we receive from our friends and relatives, his gift is not something we relegate to the closet after Christmas is past or haul out for use only now and then. Every day we need that one and only Son whom God sent so that people would not have to perish in hell but could live forever in heaven. Every day we need the Savior from sin, the source of eternal life with our Father in heaven. And even if we don't use God's Christmas gift every day, that doesn't mean we don't need it. It only means that we foolishly take it for granted or don't feel our need for it. God help us treasure his practical gift every day.

Think back to the Christmas gifts you received last year or the year before. How many do you still have left? How many do you still use? Christmas gifts have a way of wearing out, don't they? Or we simply grow weary of them. At any rate, they disappear—some more quickly than others.

Now look once again at God's Christmas gift to us. Look at how long it has lasted. Mary had it; so did the shepherds. Our parents had it; so do we. Our children have it; so will our grandchildren—at least, we hope so. Here's a gift that's permanent. It's a gift that will last to the end of days. And we pray that it will last for us till the end of our days. We want God's Christmas gift to remain ours until he takes us to eternal life in all its fullness in heaven.

When we open our Christmas gifts or which of them we remember doesn't really matter. What does matter is that we remember the personal, practical, permanent Christmas gift God gave. What does matter is that the Savior is the best Christmas present we receive every year.

Lord, there are gifts—and then there are gifts. Help us appreciate what loved ones give us this season. Above all, help us treasure your gift of the Savior, not only this Christmas Day but every day. No matter how often we have unwrapped your present, let us rejoice again today and be glad in the Savior you gave for us. Amen.

26 DEC

She gave birth to her firstborn, a son. She wrapped him in cloths and placed him in a manger, because there was no room for them in the inn. (Luke 2:7)

CHRISTMAS STILL TODAY

It all sounds so modern, doesn't it? The whole Christmas story, though many years past and many miles distant, could have happened today. We read that people had to be enrolled for taxation purposes—even as we wonder about new tax laws and what they will mean for us. We see Mary and Joseph on the road from Nazareth to Bethlehem—even as we observe how crowded our highways are at this time of the year. We notice that all the rooms were rented and there was no space left for an expectant mother—even as we try to survive in our cash-and-carry kind of world.

It could have happened today. Between that first Christmas and ours today, a number of similarities can be drawn.

One of the most disturbing similarities is that so many people still have so little room in their hearts for the Christ. Of course, they know something about why he came. Of course, they celebrate his birthday. Of course, they use his name again and again in their holiday greetings. But they have so little room for him in their me-first, care-crowded, thing-concerned hearts.

It can happen to us too! We can become so wrapped up in things like taxes and credit cards, so involved in the travel of everyday life, so engrossed in making a living and saving something for the future that the doors of our hearts creep shut little by little. Almost without realizing it, we have hung a sign on the front doors of our hearts, a sign that reads "no room."

This holy season it's time to listen again. It's time to sit up and pay attention as our services announce, "He sent forth Jesus, that true Redeemer; he sent forth Jesus to set me free." Yes, it's time to pray, "Prepare my heart, Lord Jesus; turn not from me aside, and help me to receive you this blessed Adventtide" (CW 14:4).

One of the most comforting similarities is that Christ still has room in his heart for us. Always there is room in his heart of love, in his kingdom of grace, in his Father's house. That's why he came to that Bethlehem crib and that Calvary cross. Nor will this blessed truth ever change. Aren't we glad that there's always room at his manger bed for a sinner to kneel? Aren't we glad that no matter how often we come, or with what we come, he's always there to assure the penitent, "Take heart . . . your sins are forgiven" (Matthew 9:2)? Always he has room for me, the sinner!

Aren't we glad too that he has room for everyone? Not to some queen in a palace, surrounded by servants, but to the virgin wife of a poor carpenter in the squalor of a stable was he born. Clearly, emphatically, and mercifully, this tells us that he has come for all. In a world that often recognizes only the high and the mighty and values only the rich and the famous, we need to know that Christ is for all. We may go unnoticed and unappreciated in the world; people may pass us by with seldom a sideways glance. But the Savior always has room for us—for you and for me!

And aren't we glad that he always has room for the troubled? For some of us, the joy of Christmas has been dulled. We have to celebrate without a loved one or with a load of pain. Our future is clouded over because of the circumstances in which we find ourselves. But he knows! And he always has room for the troubled.

This season it's time to thrill again. It's time, as we kneel at the manger bed, to join Paul in his joyous outburst: "Thanks be to God for his indescribable gift!" (2 Corinthians 9:15). It's time to pray, "Enter now my waiting heart, glorious King and Lord most holy. Dwell in me and ne'er depart, though I am but poor and lowly. Ah, what riches will be mine when you are my guest divine!" (CW 8:2).

Then it will be Christmas still today.

Savior Jesus, thank you for coming into our hearts this Christmas. Please dwell there and never depart. Amen.

27 DEC

When the angels had left them and gone into heaven, the shepherds said to one another, "Let's go to Bethlehem and see this thing that has happened, which the Lord has told us about." When they had seen him, they spread the word concerning what had been told them about this child. (Luke 2:15,17)

DON'T SWITCH OFF JESUS!

It was Christmas Eve. The live nativity scene had been set up in the front of the church. A lightbulb had been concealed in the straw-filled manger to make baby Jesus shine when the altar lights were extinguished. But someone hit the wrong switch and turned off all the lights—including the bulb in the manger. Out of the darkness came the plaintive voice of one of the shepherds: "Hey! You switched off Jesus!"

Switch off Jesus? Not us! We know how much we need him. Without the light of his salvation, how dark and empty our days and our eternity would be.

Those shepherds out in the fields of Bethlehem that first Christmas were not very different from us. Life was tough in their day too. They had a living to make and bills to pay. They had concerns about job security and health matters. They lived in a land whose politics were often uncertain and in a world where the future was, shall we say, unstable. And they had their sins—sins that were buried deep within their consciences and yet all too often clearly visible in their daily lives. They knew about the need for peace with God—and how unattainable that peace seemed to be.

No wonder they first trembled at the appearance of that holy angel. Yet how sweet that angel's message must have soon sounded to their troubled hearts. "Come and see," the angel told them, "Come and see the One for whom the world has been waiting. Come and see the Savior, who is Christ the Lord."

This Christmas season the angel has taken on different forms. He has come to us in the form of children with happy faces and in the form of pastors in pulpit gowns. But his message is the same: "Christ the Savior is born. Come and see and thrill at what you see. Look what our loving God has given us through his Son—full forgiveness, surpassing peace, and a future home in heaven."

Thank God that message hasn't changed. But how about our reaction to it? Have we heard the Christmas message so many times that it no longer seems as fresh and vital as it once did? Does the light of salvation that shines forth from the

Christ Child's manger seem less bright? Have the words, not to mention the meaning, of the angel's blessed message receded into the background of our busy lives?

And what was the reaction of those shepherds once they had come and seen? They spread the good news of Jesus' birth. They kept on talking about him even when they got back to their flocks and families. They used their days to go and tell.

What form do those shepherds take today? Do they look like you and me—teaching our families and telling our friends? Do they look like young people—willing to prepare themselves for lives of full-time service as pastors, teachers, and staff ministers in our congregations? Do they look like those missionaries who go in our name to far-off or nearby places? Do their hands hold offerings for missions, lessons for Sunday school pupils, work tools for congregational programs? Those who see the Savior want others to see him too. Like the shepherds, we must go and tell.

Switch off Jesus? Never! He means far too much to us.

Lord Jesus, by your grace we have again heard and seen the blessed message of our salvation this Christmas. May that good news be fresh for us each day. Help us go and tell others, that they may rejoice with us in your birth. Amen.

When the angels had left them and gone into heaven, the shepherds said to one another, "Let's go to Bethlehem and see this thing that has happened, which the Lord has told us about." So they hurried off and found Mary and Joseph, and the baby, who was lying in the manger. When they had seen him, they spread the word concerning what had been told them about this child, and all who heard it were amazed at what the shepherds said to them. The shepherds returned, glorifying and praising God for all the things they had heard and seen, which were just as they had been told. (Luke 2:15-18,20)

AN ENDLESS CHRISTMAS

"Can it be Christmas again today?" asked little Ben as he came down the steps from his bedroom. Though the family had been up late on Christmas Day, enjoying the presents and the party, Ben still woke up early. Such fun—at least so he thought— ought to be repeated day after day. And that's true! While the world has started packing its idea of Christmas away, the essentials of Christmas are ongoing for believers. Every day it's time to observe and celebrate Christmas. A brief look at how the shepherds did so will convince us that we too want an endless Christmas.

The shepherds to whom the angel preached the first Christmas sermon recognized good news when they heard it. They knew they were sinners who deserved only punishment from a just and holy God. Witness how they couldn't even stand without shivering before God's holy angels that night. They were also aware of how much they needed a Savior to bring them peace from God— peace found only in sins forgiven and heaven reopened. All this, the angel said, was there for them in that baby in Bethlehem's manger. The shepherds believed that great good news. By God's grace they knelt in worship before the manger bed. With God-given eyes of faith they saw in the Christ Child their Savior from sin. Do you think that ended their Christmas joy? Or did they, in faith, embrace the Christ Child the rest of their days?

For us Christmas is now several days removed. Though the outward trappings were different, the essentials of Christmas were the same for us as they were for the shepherds. We heard the same saving message. We know how much we need it. And we know what to do with it. By God's grace, just as for the shepherds, our Christmas joy in the Savior is not something to be closeted away with the ornaments for another year. For us the good news of Jesus is something that brings us joy every day.

107

The shepherds to whom the angel preached the first Christmas sermon might have found all sorts of excuses not to go and see Jesus. "Who'll take care of the sheep?" they might have pleaded. "How will we find him in the dark?" they might have wondered. But that's not the reaction they had. "Let's go" was their response to the angel's message. And they all went, hurrying to his manger bed so they could worship the babe of Bethlehem. Do you think that ended their worship of the Savior, or did they find ways to worship him the rest of their days?

Many of us have fond memories of the Christmas services in which we participated as children. Even now, as we watch our children or grandchildren proclaim the Christmas message, the joy comes rushing back. Let that joy continue as we whole-heartedly participate in the weekly worship services our churches put before us. Those who worship Christ in heartfelt faith will, like the shepherds, find the joy of an endless Christmas.

The shepherds to whom the angel preached that first Christmas sermon found another way to keep Christmas going. They shared it. Wherever they went, they "spread the word." Even when they returned to their flock and took up their shepherds' staffs again, they didn't stop talking about the Christ Child, whom they had worshiped with joy. When joy is spread, it's doubled, not diminished.

There's no other Christmas gift we can give away and still keep. May we find out, by experience, that the more we share the Savior with others, the more we have him ourselves. He's a Christmas gift we can give every day.

Can it be Christmas again today? Yes, today and every day, until the final and eternal day when our joy in the Savior and our worship of him will be complete.

Thank you, Lord, for the joy of Christmas, which you have given us in the Savior. Keep that joy fresh in our hearts every day. Amen.

Thanks be to God for his indescribable gift.
(2 Corinthians 9:15)

WE GOT THE GIFT; HE GETS THE PRAISE

Gifts often mean more when they are handmade by people who love us. When one of our sons was in fourth grade, he made a very special gift for me. It was a wooden, hand-punched nameplate for my desk. And it took him a great deal of time to make it. For many years I kept that gift on the desk in my study. When members would ask about it, I would proudly and gladly reply, "Mark made that for me." I got the gift, but Mark got the praise.

Isn't it the same with our Christmas gift from God? We got the gift—a gift so special that Paul calls it indescribable—but God deserves the praise. The gift is entirely of God's own making. He "handmade" it, planning, preparing, and then presenting it to us. And the love behind that gift— an indescribable love, indeed! What but God's love could bring him down from a heavenly throne to a grimy stable, from the company of holy angels to the company of sinful people and smelly animals? What but divine love could move him whose power forms baby after baby to become such a helpless baby himself?

Why did he do it? Why did God come to earth to be born as a baby? We know the answer—but it bears repeating. He was born in a manger to die on a cross as the payment for our sins. Think of the Christ Child: His little hands would one day bleed for the wrongs and failures of our hands. His tiny feet would one day be pierced with nails for wayward steps we took. His little tongue would one day burn in pain on the cross for every sinful word we've spoken. His small head would one day wear the thorns for our wicked, evil thoughts. His tender heart would one day agonize and stop beating so that our sins might be paid for and we could have peace again with God. There he was, so newly born, come to die, so that sinners like us, who could only die, might live forever with him in heaven.

God's gift of the Savior deserves more than to be kept on the desktops of our lives. The Savior wants to live in our hearts. He wants and deserves top ranking there every day. When people ask why he means so much to us, we will want to be ready with the answer, "God made him for me." And we want to be ready to add the next sentence: "He's your gift too—handmade by the same loving God, just for you."

We got the gift. But God gets the praise. How? By doing what we did this past season, of course.

It's no coincidence that some of the best and most meaningful music the world has ever heard was composed in honor of the Savior's birth. Each of us has his or her favorite hymns, and Christmas just wouldn't be complete without singing them. But why should we stop there? Getting up and going to worship services tells the world, rather visibly, what the Christ Child means to us. Singing fitting hymns for the seasons of the church year, even when a voice rumbles like a toad or screeches like an owl, offers praise to our God of love and honors his blessed name.

We give God the praise for his indescribable gift also by bringing our gifts to him. Reading the verses earlier from 2 Corinthians, we discover that Paul was talking about bringing offerings for the Lord's work. If our offering envelopes could speak, hopefully they would say, "I'm here not because my church needs money or I feel obligated to bring something but because I want to say thank you to God for his gift to me." Our offerings could hardly be called indescribable, but they can measure proportionately how ready we are to say, "I got the gift, but God gets the praise."

There are so many ways we can give God the praise. Each of us—wherever God has planted us—can grow blossoms of praise for the Lord. Parents and children want to be *Christian* parents and children. Spouses and workers want to be *Christian* spouses and workers. Members of churches and citizens of countries want to be

Christian members and citizens. Whatever we do in thought, word, or action can be our way of joining the Christmas angels in their "glory to God in the highest."

Our son Mark is long gone from home, and the nameplate he made for me has been lost somewhere in the shuffle of life. Not God's Christmas gift! We still have it, and we still want God to have the praise for it.

Lord, what a Christmas gift of salvation your love has sent us, one for us to treasure every day! Help us give you the praise for this indescribable gift with our voices and our lives. In Jesus' name we ask it. Amen.

All men are like grass, and all their glory is like the flowers of the field; the grass withers and the flowers fall, but the word of the Lord stands forever. (1 Peter 1:24,25)

CONNECTING THE EVERLASTING

"Good until 1-30-02," said the coupon for a pizza special. After that date it wasn't valid and the pizza place wouldn't deliver two pizzas for the price of one. "Use before 7-15-02," said the small print on the barbecue sauce label. Even with all the additives, the shelf life of that sauce was limited.

Ever stop to think that there are really only two things in this world that have no end: God's Word and each human being. There's no shelf life or expiration date for either one. But there had better be a connecting of the two. And that's a thought for us, as we come closer to the end of one year and the beginning of another.

Need we prove that God's Word is everlasting? "The grass withers and the flowers fall, but the word of the Lord stands forever," was the way

Peter put it. Nor was he the first to say it. He was quoting what the prophet Isaiah had written years earlier (40:8). These words take us back to late fall when Jack Frost's blasts wilted the flowers and withered the grass. But for God's Word, there is never a fall season, never a time when it withers or passes away.

Jesus, the living Word, said it too. "Heaven and earth will pass away," he told his disciples that first Holy Week, "but my words will never pass away" (Matthew 24:35). Even something that seems as enduring as the ground beneath our feet and the sky above our heads will have an end, but not a single one of his words will.

What a thought for us at the changing of the years. God's Word is everlasting. The verses we read, the Scripture we hear, the lessons we teach our children are what parents, grandparents, and great-grandparents have heard and taught. Even if we, through some folly or failure, throw away God's Word, it still will not disappear. Somehow God will see to it that it is proclaimed somewhere to someone until the end of time.

The promises in his Word are also everlasting. When God says that he has covered sin's debt, canceled sin's power, and opened heaven's door, that holds true forever. When God says that whoever believes in his Son will not perish but have eternal life, that will not change. When God says that everyone who does not believe in his Son will be damned, no passing of time or pleading of circumstances can change that either. When God says that those who hear and keep his Word can expect his blessings, that will prove as true in the year ahead as in the year past.

Mankind is also everlasting. God did not create us to die but to live forever. And so we shall. The big question is *where*. Some dispute hell's existence. They would rather close their eyes and wish away a hell where unbelievers will spend eternity. But Scripture says too much about the endless suffering, about the dwelling place of the devil and all his followers, about being cast away from God's presence forever into darkness, for us to deny hell's reality.

Others wrinkle up their noses with skepticism at the news of an eternity in heaven. But again, Scripture is very clear about being forever with the Lord, about seeing him face-to-face, about sharing his kingdom. Scripture is just as clear that only those who die in faith in Jesus as their only Savior will enjoy eternity with the Lord.

Man is no cardboard carton to be used for a while and then tossed aside into a landfill. He is no biodegradable item that only returns to the dust from which he came. God made him a body and soul that will live forever. Once again, the big question is *where*. The even bigger question is *how*. We know the answers. Thank God we know that believers in Christ Jesus will live forever in heaven. Thank God we know that such belief or faith is worked by the Spirit through the everlasting Word of God.

What greater assurance can we have as we end one year and begin another? What greater encouragement can we have for rolling up our sleeves and using the new year to connect the everlasting Word with everlasting people?

Lord, for your Word and its nourishment this past year, we thank you. Please keep us in your Word in the days ahead so that we are ready for everlasting life at your side. Amen.

Jesus Christ is the same yesterday and today and forever. (Hebrews 13:8)

NOTHING'S CHANGED

What a feeling in the pit of my stomach. Home on vacation from my church work in Canada, I drove by the old farm that my dad had sold to the city's industrial development committee. Nothing was left! All the buildings had been razed so factories could be erected. Though my parents had told me about it, I wasn't really ready for the change.

Life is full of changes. Some we welcome. Others we wince at. Some we look for. Others we lament. In one area, though, thank God there's never any change. How could we think of welcoming a new year tomorrow if we didn't have the divine assurance that with Jesus nothing has changed?

His pardon will be the same. The serious person, when changing the calendar, can't help but look back. When he does, what he sees is not all that pleasant—nasty thoughts, evil words, loveless actions. What if the Lord were to present to us today the sum total of all the sins we committed this past year? What if he would open our eyes to see all our nasty thoughts like blowing pieces of paper, all our evil words like shattered glass, all our loveless actions like dirtied plastic containers littering the ditches of the year gone by?

Who will pick up all that ugly debris? Not just bag it and haul it away to a landfill somewhere but eliminate it forever? Jesus will. Jesus has. On Calvary's cross God's own Son plunged our sins into the depths of the sea. On Calvary's cross his precious blood paid for all our sins. That payment still stands. It was our assurance throughout the past year. It will also be our assurance for years to come. For our Jesus does not change. When we come to him with our failures and faults, we don't need to wonder: "Will he forgive me yet another time? Will he tell me that I've used up my quota of forgiveness and show me to the door? Has he changed his mind about the necessary pardon for my sins?" Thank God that nothing's changed. Jesus is there with the same pardon yesterday, today, and forever.

Years change and so does life. What will the years ahead bring? It could happen that our journey will be uneventful—that the waves will be only ripples and the bumps will be only minor on this journey we call life. It could be that the waves will rock the boat and the bumps will wreck the steering. It could even be that the journey will end in the coming year. Who knows?

This much we do know: Jesus will not change. He will go with us, always at our side. When clouds cover the winter sky, we know the sun has not stopped shining. It's just that we can't see its splendor because of the clouds. So it is with the troubles of life. Even in the darkest day, Jesus is still shining on us with his warmth and comfort, seeing that all things work for our good. Thank God that nothing's changed. Jesus is there with the same peace—yesterday, today, and forever.

Just as another year ends, so will our lives. Each year, in fact, each day brings us one step closer to the inevitable. We may not like to think about it, or we may even refuse to think about it, but that doesn't change the fact that life is a short story that soon reads "the end."

So what will we do? Look over our shoulders, straining to hear the grim reaper's footsteps catching up? Or look expectantly and eagerly ahead to the Jesus who promised, "Because I live, you also will live" (John 14:19)? Thank God that nothing's changed. Jesus is there with the same promise of eternal life yesterday, today, and forever.

What a feeling—when change and decay all around we see—to know that the One who walks with us does not change. Happy New Year tomorrow in, with, and because of him!

> Swift to its close ebbs out life's little day;
> earth's joys grow dim; its glories pass away.
> Change and decay in all around I see;
> O thou who changest not, abide with me!
> Amen. (CW 588:2)

"The virgin will be with child and will give birth to a son, and they will call him Immanuel"—which means, "God with us." (Matthew 1:23)

AN OLD NAME FOR A NEW YEAR

Not many parents these days choose names like Herman or Henrietta for their children. More fanciful and up-to-date names are in vogue. Not many Christians select names like Immanuel or St. Stephen for their congregations either these days. Names like Shepherd of the Valley or Victory in Christ sound more modern.

Today, as we enter a new year, we turn to an old name. It was spoken first by the prophet Isaiah seven hundred years before the Savior's birth and then by the angel only months before his birth at Bethlehem. As we face the uncertainty of the days ahead, there's abundant comfort and assurance in that name Immanuel.

What a beautiful name for our Lord, Immanuel—"God with us." Two wonderful truths are wrapped up in that name. The first is the fact that Jesus is *God*. Eliminate that truth and Jesus would be just

121

another baby. Eliminate that truth and Jesus' death 33 years later would be just another miscarriage of justice. But such has happened before and will happen again. He has to be Immanuel, *God* with us, or else we have no salvation in him and no assurance for a new year.

The second truth is the fact that Jesus is Immanuel—God *with us*. He's not far off and distant, looking down from a lofty throne. Jesus is *God with us*—on our globe, in our flesh, under our skin. To reassure us of this comforting truth, Matthew, in his gospel, records it twice—with the angel's words before Jesus' birth "God with us" and later in Jesus' own words before his ascension. "Surely I am with you always, to the very end of the age" (28:20), the victorious Savior assures believers—regardless of what year they are entering.

What does this mean for us as we enter another year? Might we sum it up in four areas? He'll be with me in my *sins*. He ought to be against me, because he is the holy one who hates sin and has to punish each one. But again and again he's with me in my sins, not to cause them but to assure me that he has already paid for each one of them. This new year he'll be there in his Word and in his Holy Supper to remind me of his forgiveness and to assure me that I can still stand beside him in peace.

He'll be with me in my *sorrows*. How many of us had sorrow and suffering this past year? How many of us will have them this coming year? Our loving Lord does not intend sorrow's weight to bend and break us but, rather, to build up faith's fiber. Satan would whisper, sometimes even shout, that God has deserted us, but those who treasure the name Immanuel know better. Jesus has promised: "Do not fear, for I am with you; do not be dismayed, for I am your God. I will strengthen you and help you; I will uphold you with my righteous right hand" (Isaiah 41:10).

He'll be with me in my *service* to him. We know that we are to serve him with our lives. We want to give him such service. But we also remember what happened in the year gone by. So often we were weak and grew weary. At times it seemed as if we took three steps forward and five steps backward. So we wonder, even worry, whether it'll be much different in the new year. Then remember how the Savior came to Paul at Corinth when he was ready to throw in the towel. "Do not be afraid; keep on speaking, do not be silent. For I am with you," Jesus reassured him (Acts 18:9,10). Jesus not only walks alongside but promises to work with us.

He'll be with me in the *separations* of life. Know anything about the final separation—the one we call death? It came for some beside us this past year. It will also come for some of us, perhaps this very year that is unfolding now before us. But think what it means to be able to say even while we walk in the valley of the shadows, "I will fear no evil, for you are with me" (Psalm 23:4).

It's a new year, but an old name—Immanuel—equips us well for it.

Today, Lord, we thank you for the blessings of the year gone by. Help us enter this new year with the assurance that you are Immanuel—God with us—in all the areas of life. Then it will be a blessed new year for us. Amen.

2 JAN

But Mary treasured up all these things and pondered them in her heart. (Luke 2:19)

MARY'S SCRAPBOOK

Over the years my 90-year-old mother-in-law has put together many scrapbooks. Recently, as she was sorting through her earthly possessions, Grandma sent some of those books home with my wife. How interesting it proved to look back over the years and note the changes in the prices of food, cars, homes, taxes. It was even more interesting to read through the wedding write-ups of family members and the bulletin announcements of congregational events of years gone by.

Did Mary, the mother of Jesus, have a scrapbook? Did she save a corner of his cradle cloths or one of his synagogue school report cards, if they had such in that day? We aren't told. But we do know that she kept a scrapbook in her heart. More than any other mother, she had much to think about and treasure.

How often, as she diapered and nursed her baby, did the angel's words come back to her? "You are

125

to give him the name Jesus. . . . The holy one to be born will be called the Son of God" (Luke 1:31,35). How this could all be was, of course, beyond her understanding. Her mortal mind could not comprehend how God could become man and go about saving people from their sins. Nevertheless, Mary pasted those blessed words in the scrapbook of her heart and pondered them regularly.

Also in Mary's scrapbook were the words her cousin Elizabeth had spoken to her when she had hurried to Elizabeth's house with the good news of her pregnancy: "Why am I so favored, that the mother of my Lord should come to me?" (Luke 1:43). Elizabeth knew what Mary's baby would be, and so did her unborn son, John. And both shared Mary's joy.

The shepherds took up another page in her remembrances. Kneeling before her newly born son, they had related, with awe and wonder, how angels had filled the sky above them and told them about Mary's child. Then there was Simeon in the temple. She never forgot how that stranger swept her baby out of her arms and sang with joy of the salvation God had prepared for all people. Somewhere in her remembrances, she also reserved a page for the wise men, who had told her about the mysterious star from the east and then had presented their gifts to her baby and their King. So many pages made up the scrapbook of her heart— so much for her to treasure and ponder.

Not only did Mary ponder, but she also believed. With a childlike faith that comes only from the Spirit, she responded to Gabriel, "I am the Lord's servant. . . . May it be to me as you have said" (Luke 1:38). In the temple courts, where she had found her supposedly lost 12-year-old boy, she was content with his answer, "Didn't you know I had to be in my Father's house?" (Luke 2:49). At the beginning of his ministry, she told the servants at the wedding in Cana, "Do whatever he tells you" (John 2:5). As her Son neared the end of his earthly life, she stood, almost alone, beneath his cross while others shivered far away in fear. Mary had so much in the scrapbook of her heart, and through it the Spirit led her to treasure her Son as her Savior.

As we flip through the pages of Mary's scrapbook, we can't help but think of our own lives. Not all that many, like my mother-in-law, have faded items pasted on yellowing pages between two covers. But all of us have moments to remember. Like that day at the baptismal font, when Mary's son put his cross upon our foreheads and our breasts, in token that we had been redeemed by him. Like those moments at the supper table, when Jesus spoke to us through the family devotions led by our parents. Like our confirmation day, when we spoke vows we could not keep to a Savior who would forgive us when we failed and fire us up to try again. Like our kneeling at the Communion table, when his very body and blood were given to assure us that we are still his forgiven brothers and sisters, whose names are still written on rooms in his Father's house.

Scrapbooks of the heart—hopefully we all have them. Hopefully we all take time to turn to them and treasure Mary's son, our blessed Savior, on each page.

Thank you for the miracle of Jesus' birth through the virgin Mary. Help us, as you did her, to treasure him as our Savior and each day to think with joy about what you have given us in him. Amen.

Simeon took him in his arms and praised God,
saying: "Sovereign Lord, as you have promised, you
now dismiss your servant in peace. For my eyes
have seen your salvation, which you have prepared
in the sight of all people, a light for revelation to
the Gentiles and for glory to your people Israel."
(Luke 2:28-32)

HOLDING OR HELD?

It was the day of her baptism. After dinner, as I
was cradling my granddaughter in my chair, she
fell sound asleep. I didn't want to move even a
muscle as she, totally relaxed, almost melted onto
my chest. Megan doesn't remember that after-
noon, but I do, and the wonderful feelings I asso-
ciate with holding her.

That day in the temple, Simeon also held a baby.
The feelings he had as he held Jesus far surpassed
what I felt holding Megan. Those feelings were
made even more wonderful because Simeon realized that the baby he was holding was actually
holding him.

We don't know much about the man who swept the baby Jesus out of Mary's arms that day in the temple. He appears only here in Scripture and with little detail. But we do know whom he was holding to his chest. Simeon knew it too. God's Holy Spirit had revealed to him that "he would not die before he had seen the Lord's Christ" (Luke 2:26). The same Spirit led him to the temple that day, to the holy family, and to the baby in his arms. Best of all, the Spirit led him to see in that baby the salvation God had promised.

Can we imagine Simeon's feelings as he held the Savior in his arms? He was holding God in human flesh. He was cradling forgiveness in person. He was embracing the answer to all his hopes and fears. We can almost imagine him squeezing the baby Jesus just a little tighter as he sang his joyful hymn of praise.

Don't you wish you could take Simeon's place? We can! The same Spirit makes it possible for us to hold the Christ Child, not with our arms, of course, but with our hearts. Faith's arms may be invisible, but the Savior they hold is very real. Nor should our joy be any less than Simeon's. This past Christmas season has been a special time for holding the Savior even more closely to our hearts. Pray to God that we used it. Thank God for the heightened joy it brought us.

With eyes of faith, Simeon saw more than the Christ Child he was holding. He saw the Christ Child holding him. That's why he could speak so peacefully about death. His words "You now dismiss your servant in peace" don't sound much like the abject fear the world connects with the monster it calls death. They sound more like the confession of a man who is ready for discharge from service on earth and who is eager for enlistment in heaven's ranks. They come from someone who knows whose loving arms are wrapped around him and who trusts those powerful arms to hold him even into eternity.

So do we! That's also part of our Christmas joy. Mary's baby was born to die, so that we, who can only die, may live forever. The Prince of life gave up his life to give us life that never ends. Behind the crib stands the cross, and behind the cross, the cure for death. But only those whom Jesus holds in his arms know this and are safe. Thank God his arms are around us. Pray God this blessed truth will bring us never-ending joy.

Jesus' arms are big enough to hold the whole dying world. Simeon recognized this and described the Savior as a "revelation to the Gentiles and for glory to your people Israel." Whether Simeon had time left to tell others about death's only remedy, we aren't told. But we still have time. Whom have we told this past Christmas season? Whom will we tell today?

Holding or held? Both—thank God! Because of his grace, we hold Jesus and are held by him! We surely wouldn't want it any other way.

Be near me, Lord Jesus; I ask you to stay close by me forever and love me, I pray. Bless all the dear children in your tender care, and take us to heaven to live with you there. Amen. (CW 68:3)

4 JAN

There was also a prophetess, Anna, the daughter of Phanuel, of the tribe of Asher. She was very old; she had lived with her husband seven years after her marriage, and then was a widow until she was eighty-four. She never left the temple but worshiped night and day, fasting and praying. Coming up to them at that very moment, she gave thanks to God and spoke about the child to all who were looking forward to the redemption of Jerusalem. (Luke 2:36-38)

WORSHIPER AND WITNESS

Laura never made it into any listings of the great and famous, but she was number one in my book. Though troubled with recurring health problems, she seldom missed a worship service. The fourth pew from the front was her spot on Sundays. Laura also never hesitated telling others about the Savior she loved. "Pastor, come quick," she telephoned one day. "I've got the Culligan delivery man in my kitchen, and I need some help telling him about Jesus."

Makes me think about Anna. Her biography is one of the briefest in the Bible—only three short

133

verses. But from her comes an illustration of life's purpose—to know Jesus for ourselves and to help others know him.

Anna was a woman who seemed to have gotten little out of life and had little left of life. After only seven years of marriage, her husband had died. For a good share of her 84 years, she had been left alone to face a life that could have been tough and empty. But Anna was not sad. Instead of complaining about her lot in life or wearing out her days in whining, she spent them worshiping and working in the temple. God's house became her spiritual home. Within its walls she received strength for her own life and set an example for others. Like Mary who sat at Jesus' feet, Anna chose the better part that could not be taken away from her. Then, like Martha, she busied herself serving her Savior in whatever way she could.

One day as Anna worshiped and served in the temple, she found what she had been looking for. She, like Simeon, was privileged to see the Lord's salvation. She, like Simeon, gave thanks to the Lord. And, like Simeon, she could now depart in peace. Just think how much she would have missed if she had neglected going to the temple that day.

"Don't preach so much about those who don't come to worship," a parishioner once told me after a service. "Tell those of us who were here how good it is for us to come," he urged. He was right. Let others pass by opportunities to hold their Savior; Anna didn't. Let others fail to sing the praises of the Father's love in sending the Christ Child; Anna didn't. Let others imagine themselves too busy to give thanks to God for the immense gift of salvation; Anna didn't. Let others ignore the fueling for a life of faith that comes only from the good news of Jesus; Anna didn't. Nor will you or I! Instead, we'll join Anna and Laura in regularly worshiping our Lord and Savior.

And in telling others about him. Anna "spoke about the child to all who were looking forward to the redemption of Jerusalem." The worshiper became a witness. That's how it works. Christ in the arms of faith becomes Christ on the tongues of faith. Anna couldn't keep the good news to herself. She had to tell others. At age 84 she became one of the first missionaries. What a beautiful way to come to the end of life, using the days left to tell others about the only Savior and way to heaven.

Did you notice where Anna did her witnessing? Right where the Lord had placed her—in Jerusalem, to those around her. The home is a woman's special mission field. She influences little hearts, folds little hands, fills little ears. She has more impact than she sometimes realizes on her husband and on her growing children as she quietly models faith in the affairs of daily life. Not only did many of us learn much about Jesus from our mothers, but we also learned much about serving Jesus from them.

It makes no difference whether our names are Anna or Laura or whatever. What does matter is that we view life as a time of God's grace for us to know Jesus and help others know him too. Then our names will be written not in the annals of the rich and famous but in God's book of life in heaven—all because of Jesus!

Thank you, Lord, for bringing us to Jesus. Help us live in your Word so that we get to know him even better. Help us tell others about him in any way that we can, so that they can join us in worshiping and praising you. In his name we ask it. Amen.

5 JAN

After this I looked and there before me was a great multitude that no one could count, from every nation, tribe, people and language, standing before the throne and in front of the Lamb. They were wearing white robes and were holding palm branches in their hands. And they cried out in a loud voice: "Salvation belongs to our God, who sits on the throne, and to the Lamb." (Revelation 7:9,10)

WE WANT TO BE IN THAT NUMBER

"That's what he looks like to me," said the Nigerian Christian. The hand-carved crucifix he had given me showed Jesus with African features. When I politely asked why, such was his answer. Though he knew Jesus was a descendant of David's line, that Christian pictured Jesus as his brother, come in his flesh, to save him. What a lesson it was for me about the scope of Jesus' salvation.

Sometimes we limit the Savior. "My Savior," we label him, perhaps adding, "my spouse's Savior and my children's Savior." Maybe once in a while we even add, "My neighbor's Savior too." Nor are we wrong. Jesus is all that—but he is also so much more. He is the Savior of all people. He wants all people to know him as we do. And he wants us to tell all people about him.

Some days I can hardly wait to be part of the heavenly scene John describes for us. With perfect hearts and voices, we'll join the heavenly hosts in singing our Savior-God's praises. The most resounding Easter service that we ever participated in here in this world will seem like only a warm-up compared to the worship we'll take part in above. The crowd at a Reformation rally or special anniversary service will seem like only a handful when contrasted to the heavenly multitude. Some of the people will be like you and me, but a great many more will be different. In the multitude will be people from every nation, tribe, people, and language.

Yet in one most important respect, we'll all be the same. We'll be there because of the Lamb. We'll be there because of the salvation that belongs to our God. We'll be there because his love planned, prepared, and then brought his salvation to each one of us. Together our one object of attention will be the One on the throne and his Lamb. Together our one object of worship will be the Lord, whose love and grace have brought us to him.

I want to be in that number. Don't you? Thank God someone told us about the Lamb. Thank God for Christian parents and grandparents, husbands and wives, teachers and pastors, neighbors and acquaintances who wanted us to be in that number. Thank God for the good news of Jesus they shared and keep sharing with us. Through their witnessing, God's love and grace worked to add and keep us in that number.

While we're waiting to join that heavenly scene, there's work for us to do. We might even call this work all important, because that's how God rates it. Of course, we get an education and hold a job. We pay our bills and use part of the extra to have fun. We get married and look forward to children and grandchildren. We philosophize about making the world a better place for those who follow us. We strive for peaceful existence with our neighbors next door and across the world. But what is all this if that's all there is? These are nickels and dimes God gives to help us live. We are not to be held hostage by them. God's reason for still leaving us here on earth is far deeper. He leaves us here to witness about the Lamb so that others may join us in that heavenly multitude.

Sometimes at night, thinking ahead to that eternal day, I pray, "Please, Lord, let me be in that number. Please, Lord, let my wife and our four children be in that number too. Please, Lord, let our six grandchildren be in that number also. And please, Lord, if it's not too much to ask, could I see in that number one or two more to whom you used me to witness."

Me in that number? Pray God that it be so. Others in that number? Pray God would put us to work and bless our efforts.

Let none hear you idly saying, "There is nothing I can do," while the multitudes are dying, and the Master calls for you. Take the task he gives you gladly; let his work your pleasure be. Answer quickly when he calleth, "Here am I—send me, send me!" Amen. (CW 573:4)

6 JAN

On coming to the house, they saw the child with his mother Mary, and they bowed down and worshiped him. Then they opened their treasures and presented him with gifts of gold and of incense and of myrrh. (Matthew 2:11)

A WORD FROM THE WISE

"A word from the wise," an old proverb says, "is sufficient." We ought to listen to those who know what they are talking about. Are you ready for a word from the wise? What would the wise men of old say to us? What would they have us remember? Very simply, they might point us to Jesus and say, "Seek him and serve him."

"We weren't the ones you might have expected," those wise men might begin. "The shepherds who heard the angels, the people of Bethlehem to whom the news filtered down—you might have expected to find them kneeling before him. But that day, when we dismounted before the house where he was sheltered, we created quite a stir. We were strangers from a faraway land, Gentiles having nothing to do with Abraham's seed. How Bethlehem must have buzzed that day."

"And you," the wise men might continue, pointing to us, "how do you fit in?"

"Oh, we've always been here," most of us would answer. "We aren't Jews either. But unlike you wise men, we've had the Savior for so long that we sometimes take him for granted."

Perhaps those wise men should remind us again how fortunate we are. God's grace has brought us, just as he brought them, to the house where the Christ Child dwells. For them it was the living Word in that house. For us it is the written Word in our houses of God and in our homes. Let those wise men remind us how fortunate we are to have the Savior and how we must not rest "till each remotest nation has learned Messiah's name."

"He didn't look like much," they might continue, "just a little boy in the arms of a humble maiden. But to our eyes of faith, he looked like everything. There he was, the one we were looking for, our Savior, our Lord. Can you imagine how we felt when we knelt before him? *Overjoyed* is a word that comes to mind."

"And you," the wise men might continue, pointing to us, "what does he mean to you?" Yes, what does Jesus mean to us? The answer has a direct bearing on how hard we will seek him. If we believe that God punishes every sin and that hell's fires are still burning, and if we believe that he is our only ticket—fully paid and freely given—to heaven, we will seek him. If we know that we cannot live without him—that life's burdens are too heavy, that life's temptations are too forceful and life's sorrows too stifling—then a word from the wise ought to be sufficient. Then we'll use this new year to seek him.

And to serve him. "We brought the best we had," the wise men might remind us, "gold fit for a king, incense and myrrh, still precious and still used in perfumes in your day. Our gifts were nothing small or sparing. How could they be? We were bringing them to our Savior."

"And you," the wise men might continue, pointing at us, "what kind of gifts do you bring from your treasure chests?" "No," they might remind us, "you can't say that such things shouldn't be talked about, that enough sermons are preached about giving already, that everybody knows the times are tough." "What we are saying," they might continue, "is that faith gives not from the bottom but from the top of the wealth God gives."

"And you," they might continue, pointing at us, "what kind of service did you render your King last year? How many of the 8,760 hours of the past year did you dedicate to him? How many will you give him this year, whether you are a newly elected church board member, a family person, an employer, an employee, a teacher, or a pastor? That's how it goes with a believer," they might say. "He serves his Savior with the best he has."

A word from the wise, they say, is sufficient. God, make it so!

Thank you, Lord, for numbering us with the wise. Eyes of faith to see, hearts of faith to treasure, and hands of faith to serve the Redeemer King come from you. Keep us wise through faith in Christ, and keep us ready for his service in all the days before us this new year. Amen.